"From the Silence
of Tao House"

"From the Silence of Tao House"

ESSAYS ABOUT
EUGENE & CARLOTTA O'NEILL
AND THE TAO HOUSE PLAYS

by

Travis Bogard

THE EUGENE O'NEILL FOUNDATION :: TAO HOUSE
POST OFFICE BOX 402   DANVILLE   CALIFORNIA 94526

ISBN 0-9637215-1-8 QUALITY PAPERBACK
ISBN 0-9637215-0-X CLOTHBOUND

Front Cover Photo :: Tao House © 1989 Chris Duffey
Back Cover, Author Photo :: © William S. Murphy

Creative Direction :: Pennfield Jensen
Book Design & Typography :: George Mattingly
Printed by PENN & INK through Colorcraft, Ltd., Hong Kong

for Darlene Blair and Lois Sizoo

Good friends, great O'Neillians

(ABOVE) :: EUGENE O'NEILL, 1938. REPRODUCED COURTESY OF BETTMANN NEWSPHOTOS.

Contents

A Letter from Jason Robards

It has been a privilege to have known Professor Emeritus Travis Bogard of the University of California, Berkeley for many years. He is recognized as an important scholar of the works and life of Eugene O'Neill and has served us all by editing the three volume collection of the dramatist's complete plays and, in a parallel volume, his major unpublished works. His seminal critical study, *Contour in Time, the Plays of Eugene O'Neill* created a bond between us twenty years ago. We have both spent a major portion of our lives interpreting O'Neill's plays, he in his classes and publications, I on the stage. That bond has been strengthened through a series of meetings at O'Neill's California home, Tao House.

In 1975, the newly organized Eugene O'Neill Foundation, Tao House, requested that I give a benefit performance of *Hughie* to help them raise funds to purchase the house and save it from developers. Bogard agreed to help with the production facilities through the University's drama department in Zellerbach Hall on the campus. The audience was so encouraging that Jack Dodson and I continued the run later that summer at the Westwood Playhouse in Los Angeles for the benefit of The Foundation.

With the proceeds, The Foundation was able to acquire title to the property and begin showing the house to the public. The next year, the California legislature agreed to complete the purchase of Tao House for later transfer to the National Government as a National Historic Site. It is entirely fitting that Tao House be part of the federal government's memorial holdings. O'Neill is a giant of the American drama and remains to this day the only playwright to have been awarded the Nobel Prize for Literature.

The contributions of Travis Bogard to their successful venture and to the cause of O'Neill cannot be measured. I am certain that Foundation members will agree that none of this could have happened without his impeccable artistic sense, expertise and commitment.

This book, a compilation of his essays over the past quarter century on O'Neill and his plays, exemplifies his sensitive understanding and appreciation of the genius of America's greatest playwright.

I am honored to play this small role in its publication.

Jason Robards

A Prefatory Note

This book has been prepared as a gift to the Eugene O'Neill Foundation, Tao House for such aid as it may prove to be in the development of programs for the dramatist's western home. Tao House, located in California's San Ramon Valley above the town of Danville, is now, through the efforts of the Foundation a National Historic Site. The National Park Service manages with great care and skill the restoration and maintenance of the property and arranges public tours. The Foundation is committed to creating programs appropriate to the memory of Eugene and Carlotta O'Neill and to the great creative energy O'Neill expended there.

When I first saw Tao House it bore little resemblance to what it had been when the O'Neills lived there. It had undergone a number of architectural alterations and Carlotta's assertive color scheme had been subdued. It had been rented for several years and gave ominous signs of falling into disrepair. There was talk of its being torn down so that condominiums could be built on the site. In the end, it was saved by the devoted enterprise of a few community residents who successfully brought it under the protection of the national government.

Once the safety of the property was assured, the work of devising a program for the use of the house began. In those years—the late 1970's—I invited both established performing artists and students of the performing arts to visit the house. After they had been given time to sense its qualities, I asked them to suggest what uses it might have for them.

The answers were creative and varied, but they all pointed to a common objective. Katharine Hepburn, for example, said that she had often wished for some place where she might come only to study a play. She said that when she appeared in a play it was "so expensive," by which she meant that it was committed to all the machinery of production and the difficulties of public performance. To work with no production in view on a role of personal interest with other actors ("good actors," she said firmly) would be well worthwhile. Sam Shepard said that he had no interest in the Foundation's producing his plays, but that it would be valuable to spend time at Tao House with perhaps an architect and a musician to see what kind of theatre piece they might make together. Other responses were similar—individual in detail, but all pointing to the use of the house as a retreat where formal or informal creative projects might be developed. One of my graduate students from the University of California Drama Department told me fiercely: "There's a creative spirit about this place and don't you louse it up!" Being a Berkeley student she used a more aggressive term than "louse," but her command seemed to me to summarize the charge for the enterprise we had taken in hand.

Programs at Tao House now have a clear objective: to keep alive O'Neill's presence. This has involved making his name known and valued throughout the community, and to cause the general public to realize that the Tao House plays (which include *Long Day's Journey into Night, A Moon for the Misbegotten, The Iceman Cometh, Hughie, A Touch of the Poet,* and *More Stately Mansions*) rank among the greatest contributions to world theatre. Foundation members have established a library on the site of important materials relating to O'Neill and the American theatre. They regularly open the house to young students who are introduced to O'Neill's work and invited to participate in responsive creative sessions. They arrange for productions of scenes from O'Neill in short informal hearings throughout the community, and, through lectures and exhibits, they seek to inform interested groups about O'Neill's life and works. Somewhat farther down the line, following the suggestions of early visitors, they plan to open the house to both established and beginning performing artists who may wish to use it as a retreat in order to work for a time in O'Neill's world, where they may absorb some of his creative spirit into projects of their own.

These essays have been part of the general informational program. Written over a period of twenty-five years for a variety of audiences, they are for the most part casual pieces. Inevitably from essay to essay they repeat facts and interpretations of O'Neill's work. I have reduced the repetition as far as possible, but some must remain if the coherence of the individual essay is to be preserved. For example, a reader will see such repetition in the comments on *"Anna Christie"* in the two essays, "Little Orphan *'Anna Christie'*" and "The Empowering Sea." My hope is that in the first, the close focus on the play will provide a different perspective from the view of the play in a wider context in the latter.

Some themes developed here are constant: O'Neill's "seeking flight," and the quest for belonging that was repeated as an urgency in his younger plays and as a memory in the later; the contribution of Tao House to his final, masterful accomplishment; the tragic silencing brought about by his illness; and particularly the strength of the love between O'Neill and Carlotta—a devotion that some have called in question.

This publication owes much to many. Clarence Woodard and the Woodard Foundation have made a substantially generous contribution toward its realization, as have the following board members and friends of the Eugene O'Neill Foundation, Tao House: Kathryne Radovan Albertoni, Darleen and Bill Blair, Edward M. Gibbs, Carol Lea Jones, Jerry Lar Rieu, Diane Schinnerer and Wesley and Lois Sizoo.

Jackson R. Bryer, Pennfield Jensen, Lois Sizoo and George Theodosy have provided invaluable editorial assistance. I am grateful to Patricia Willis and the American Literature Collection of the Beinecke Rare Book and Manuscript Library of Yale University for permission to quote from O'Neill's plays, poems and work diaries. I thank also the following sources for permission to quote material in their collections: from O'Neill's letters to Beatrice Ashe Mather, the Henry and Albert A. Berg Collection, the New York Public Library, Astor and Lennox Foundations; from O'Neill's correspondence with Agnes Boulton O'Neill, the Theatre Collection, The Houghton Library, Harvard University; from recordings of O'Neill's sea plays, BARD Productions, Berkeley, CA; from O'Neill's medical records, The Eugene O'Neill Foundation, Tao House.

The cover photograph of Tao House is the gift of its photographer, Chris Duffey. The photograph of O'Neill at Tao House is reproduced with the generous permission of the Bettmann Archive. The photographs of O'Neill as a student at Harvard are reproduced through the courtesy of Jere W. Hageman. The author's photograph is by William S. Murphy.

— Travis Bogard

I

About Eugene and Carlotta O'Neill

The Seeking Flight
From the Silence of Tao House
Birthday Greetings to Eugene O'Neill
O'Neill in Love
Love's Labors Dispossessed

The Seeking Flight

In his study at Tao House, like the disturbing flutter of unseen things, the past intruded on Eugene O'Neill's imagination. Memories he had tried for a lifetime to leave behind thrust themselves forward. Compounded of guilt and love and hate, they remained insistent, driving him toward the moment when he found at last that he could exorcise them and end their long pursuit.

In 1926, on a ship bound for Bermuda, O'Neill wrote nostalgically to his new-found love, the actress Carlotta Monterey. The deep swell of the Atlantic as the ship left the calm of New York harbor called back to his mind the several voyages he had made on sailing ships and freighters:

> She's starting to roll now, off the Hook. I remember in my sailor days what a thrill of life it gave me, that first feel of the great ground swell of ocean heaving under me. It meant a release then, an end of an old episode and the birth of a new. Life then was simply a series of episodes flickering across my soul like the animated drawings one sees in the movies, and I could not then see how the continuity of my own seeking flight ran through them as a sustained pattern.

The long journey that led him at last to the silent study in Tao House had been adventurous and hard. It had taken him through the depths of life to the edge of death. He had known intense love and had been filled with debilitating hatred. He had known sorrows in his immediate family that most men never face. He came at last to understand that throughout his life he had been running from something that terrified him. Yet as he looked back on his life, he came to feel that he had also been running desperately *toward* salvation, at once a fugitive and a quester on a "seeking flight."

The flight came to its end in the study of his California home, Tao House, where, as he wrote in the dedication to his play, *Long Day's Journey into Night*, he was able to face his dead. Salvation, he discovered, lay in bringing his art to assuage the guilt of the past, and in so doing to ask for and to grant forgiveness. But the discovery was to take a lifetime of search. The play he wrote of his family was the milepost that marked the end of his search. Together with the other plays written at Tao House, *Hughie, A Moon for the Misbegotten, The Iceman Cometh, A Touch of the Poet* and its sequel, the unfinished *More Stately Mansions*, it summed all that he had done before with passion and pity and wisdom.

What in his past caused a lifetime of anguished searching? Eugene was the third son of an Irish immigrant, James O'Neill, who became one of the major stars of nineteenth century theatre. James rose rapidly in the theatrical hierarchy from super to leading man, until he came to equal the great Edwin Booth in Shakespearean performances. Like all actors in the nineteenth century, he was forced to spend his life touring the country in sooty trains and dusty stage coaches, bringing theatre to the nation. Moving from hotel to hotel, his was a nomad's life which his family was forced to share. The lack of a settled world would prove disastrous to their well-being.

He at first thought his fortune was made by the acclaim he received for his performance in an adaptation of Alexandre Dumas' novel *The Count of Monte Cristo*. The play relates the story of Edmond Dantès who is falsely accused of treason and committed to the island prison, the Château d'If. The melodramatic tale tells of his lucky escape from prison, his acquisition of riches and his revenge on those who have betrayed him. The play's sensation scene occurs when Dantès is thrown from the island. Emerging from the stormy seas, he clambers upon a rock and, exulting in his freedom and fortune, cries out "Saved! Mine, the treasures of Monte Cristo! The world is mine!"

Throughout James's life, the line echoed with irony. He was

wildly successful in the romantic role, but, as has happened with many another actor, the public had no great interest in his performance in other roles but demanded that he give them *Monte Cristo*— always *Monte Cristo*. The play became a trap which gradually absorbed his creativity and stunted his talent. Although night after night he cried out "The world is mine!" the words were sour in his mouth, and embittering to his spirit.

When he began to write, Eugene delivered the death blow to such melodramatic entertainments. At first, however, he knew only that he found such claptrap drama ludicrous. He spoke once of "the theatre of my father that I hate," and that hatred in some measure set him on his flight.

His father's theatre was entwined with a desolate family story. In 1877, James married a convent-educated Connecticut girl, Mary Ellen Quinlan, who preferred to be known as "Ella." A year later, their son James Jr., affectionately known as Jamie, was born in San Francisco. Their second son, Edmund, was born in 1883, but died within two years from measles contracted from his brother. Ella's sorrow seemed inextinguishable, and her husband felt that the only remedy was for her to replace the dead baby with another child. On October 16, 1888 in a hotel room on Broadway in New York City, Eugene Gladstone was born. The birth was difficult, and in the not uncommon practice of the period, the doctor prescribed morphine to ease her pain. The danger was clear, the doctor careless, and Ella became an addict. Her addiction affected Jamie deeply, and as he grew older, he fled the reality by making the rounds of bars and brothels, a way of living to which he introduced his younger brother as soon as Eugene entered his late teens. Ella's condition had been kept from Eugene while he was young, but discovery was inevitable on the night when in a madness induced by the morphine, Ella rushed from the house and attempted to drown herself in the river flowing past their summer home, called, with a certain irony, Monte Cristo Cottage.

The cottage in New London, Connecticut was the only home that the O'Neills had. It was small, dark and somehow impermanent, and its atmosphere drove O'Neill later in life to seek out large, even stately homes, no doubt in reaction to the minimal security and comfort Monte Cristo Cottage offered.

To leave the depressing environment and the failed lives of his family, as soon as he came of age Eugene took flight in earnest. He completed preparatory school in 1906, went on to Princeton, but flunked out at the end of his first year. Thereafter he lived in the bohemian world of Greenwich Village in New York City, an aimless wanderer.

He met a young girl, Kathleen Jenkins, made her pregnant, and married her, but neither family approved of the marriage, and shortly Eugene tried again to escape, this time on a gold-prospecting expedition to Honduras. An attack of malaria occasioned his return to the United States in the spring of 1910. His son, Eugene, Jr. was born in May, but O'Neill saw his wife and the baby only once. Again in flight, he left New York, on a Norwegian sailing vessel for Buenos Aires.

The voyage became important to him later, for in several of his plays he was to write feelingly of the beauty of life at sea under sail power. He also was to see life at its lowest ebb when he left the ship in Buenos Aires and spent some time as a waterfront bum, penniless, sleeping on park benches, drinking to great excess, and once even contemplating armed robbery in order to survive.

He returned to New York in 1911 and moved to a waterfront saloon and flop-house run by James Condon, known as "Jimmy the Priest." The establishment, a down-at-the-heels haven for those who needed little beside a cheap bed and cheap whiskey, was to provide the setting and many of the characters for *"Anna Christie"* and *The Iceman Cometh.*

Restless, never at peace, late in the same year, he shipped out on a tramp freighter to England, an event he would recall when he wrote about the sailors of the S. S. *Glencairn*. Returning to New York, he arranged for a divorce from Kathleen in the then customary and unsavory way of being discovered by a detective in a hotel room with a hired companion. His disgust with life was so great that the following year, at Jimmy-the-Priest's, he attempted to commit suicide by taking an overdose of sleeping medicine.

He was saved by his room-mate. Thereafter with no clear future, he toured with the *Monte Cristo* company, playing the role of the jailer at the Château d'If and working as an assistant stage manager. In the fall he returned to New London and worked on the *Telegraph* as a reporter. For the paper he wrote occasional poems and led a life of outward normality. In December, 1912, however, there came a significant change. On Christmas Eve, he entered Gaylord Farm Sanitarium with tuberculosis.

In the sanitarium, he came to a point of rest and for the first time began to evaluate his life as a fugitive. To this point, he had lived as a desperate failure. Like his brother, who had worked haphazardly as an actor, but whose life was increasingly governed by his alcoholic dependency, Eugene seemed determined on alcoholic self-destruction. Yet what had been was not all waste. His education after preparatory school had been scanty and informal, but he read widely and intelligently. He had frequented an anarchist bookstore in New York City, where in addition to the tracts of Emma Goldman and other radical writers, he discovered the work of Henrik Ibsen, Bernard Shaw, and Friedrich Nietzsche. He read the novels of Joseph Conrad and Jack London, and he took pleasure in the dark eroticism of the fin-de-siècle poets, Charles Baudelaire, Ernest Dowson, Algernon Charles Swinburne, Oscar Wilde and Edward Fitzgerald. He went to the theatre, taking enthusiastic pleasure (he attended ten times) in the 1907 production of *Hedda Gabler* by the Russian actress Alla Nazimova who would later create the role of Christine Mannon in his *Mourning Becomes Electra*. In 1911, while he lived at Jimmy-the-Priest's he went to all the New York performances of Dublin's Abbey Theatre on their first

American tour, and learned from them a new form of poetic realism which he would soon turn to good use.

It was an informal but significant education, and while he recuperated at Gaylord Farm, (he was discharged as an "arrested" case in 1913) he continued his wide reading. It was an almost inevitable consequence, given his turn of mind and his theatrical background, that he would begin to write for the theatre. Writing gave him an aim and became an important cause of his return to health. The experience is detailed in his play about life in a tuberculosis sanitarium, *The Straw*.

The first works were tentative to the point of absurdity. In 1914, Eugene's father subsidized their printing in a volume called *Thirst and Other One-Act Plays*. The collection comprises five short plays he called "ironic tragedies," a term which means little except that most of the cast dies by a some improbable trick of fate. Although they owe something to the German drama of the late nineteenth and early twentieth centuries, they are all inexpert and show little beyond the ability to think dramatically. Yet that same year, he wrote one short play—*Bound East for Cardiff*, the story of a dying sailor on a tramp steamer, the S. S. *Glencairn*—in which he spoke with his own voice and began to develop the view that men belonged to some large force that controls their destiny. In this play, the ironic tragedy is set on a partially philosophical base and the O. Henry-like endings of other early plays are laid aside.

Bound East for Cardiff was submitted to Prof. George Pierce Baker when he applied in 1914 for admission to Harvard University so that he might enroll in the nation's first course in playwriting. A new determination spoke in his application: "I want to be an artist or nothing." The play and the new resolve served him well in 1916 when he offered it to a group of amateurs summering on Cape Cod. They staged it in a shed built out over a wharf, and in the fog with the lapping sound of the sea, the play proved exceptionally effective. Its poetic realism, reminiscent of the quality of the Abbey Theatre plays, called up for the players a vision of what they might bring to the je-june American theatre. One of their members said after seeing it, "Then we knew what we were for."

Their success at the summer amusement motivated the group to organize as "The Provincetown Players," and to open a theatre in Greenwich Village later that fall. Converting an old brownstone house into a tiny theatre, they called upon the talents of many of the writers and artists who lived in the bohemian world. Robert Edmond Jones, who became the pre-eminent American scene designer, Susan Glaspell, who would become an important playwright, Edna St. Vincent Millay, Jasper Deeter and many others contributed their time and enthusiastic talent to the work, which was led by the poet and classical scholar, George Cram Cook, serving as producer. For O'Neill, the theatre became an atelier where he could learn his craft and experiment as he chose.

He wrote rapidly during the 1920's. Plays poured from him as if they had been long bottled up. Between 1916 and 1928, he completed thirty-one plays. Some of them were in one act, but as he moved from the Village amateurs onto the stages of professional Broadway managers, they brought a new degree of serious playwriting to the American theatre. *Desire Under the Elms* blended themes from ancient Greek tragedy with Freudian understanding of character in a rural setting on a bleak New England farm. *All God's Chillun Got Wings* was concerned with an inter-racial marriage. *Strange Interlude* centered on a woman who has a baby out of wedlock in order to save her husband from madness. As the plays grew in serious subject matter, so they grew in length. The first version of *Marco Millions*, a lavish, satiric comedy about Marco Polo's voyage to China, is in eight acts; *Strange Interlude* is in nine. Ultimately O'Neill, in collaboration with Robert Edmond Jones and the critic Kenneth Macgowan took over the running of the Provincetown Playhouse and used it for experimental productions that were not the regular fare of the Broadway managements. With his colleagues, he studied advanced techniques of European dramatic art as practiced by Gordon Craig, Max Reinhardt and the Russian theatre. He became known for his startling innovations in stagecraft, such as the drums which sounded continually through the action of *The Emperor Jones* or the masks that dramatized the dual identities of the characters in *The Great God Brown*. In *Strange Interlude*, he caused the characters to speak their thoughts aloud, calling back into contemporary stage practice the almost forgotten technique of the aside and soliloquy for the purpose. In *Lazarus Laughed*, using masks, massed choruses and dance he attempted a ritual drama filled with overpowering spectacle and sound.

These plays were not mere demonstrations of technical virtuosity. Writing of the Swedish dramatist August Strindberg, he praised him for doing more than to "hold the family kodak up to ill-nature." Strindberg moved, he said, "behind life," showing the forces that underlay observable patterns of behavior. Like Strindberg, O'Neill set himself to understand the forces, the god-like essence, from which human beings came and to which they belonged. He was a renegade Catholic, and he turned away from theological orthodoxy, but his quest was in actuality a religious one. All of the plays in this period are plays in which characters seeks to come into unity with a force that both controls and protects them. Sometimes it is a force of nature, a spirit moving in the sea or the land. Thus Anna Christie comes from exile on a land-locked midwestern farm to discover that she belongs to the sea and only there can find happiness. Robert Mayo in *Beyond the Horizon* belongs to the sea, but deserts it. His apostasy costs him his life. Yank in *The Hairy Ape* belongs to the power of steam and steel and cannot survive once his allegiance to these forces is questioned.

Other forces were explored: the land in *Desire Under the Elms*, God as a mother in *Strange Interlude*, God in electricity in *Dynamo*, and even God in the Catholic church in *Days Without End*. The nature of the god-force was less important than the fact of belonging, of finding some way of sinking the restless, warring elements of human existence into a great pool of quiet, of existing simply, without consciousness. Remembering what he had felt as a younger man at sea, he caused the character who represented himself in *Long Day's Journey into Night* to describe the condition. Edmund tells of being on a sailing ship and of "dissolving" into the beauty of the night, of becoming moonlight and the ship's sails and the spray, of becoming

> the sun, the hot sand, green seaweed anchored to a rock, swaying in the tide. Like a saint's vision of beatitude. Like the veil of things as they seem drawn back by an unseen hand. For a second you see the secret—and seeing the secret are the secret. For a second there is meaning! Then the hand lets the veil fall and you are alone, lost in the fog again, and you stumble on toward nowhere for no good reason.

The technical experiments permitted him to break open the surface appearances of life and to explore the nature of divinity "behind life" in a variety of ways. Thus he was able to figure forth not the force itself but the depth and intensity of the search for vision. So it was that not only in the exciting technical achievements which introduced his audiences to a new kind of theatre, but also in the seriousness of his themes, O'Neill commanded interest and respect, manifested by the fact that he won the Pulitzer Prize for drama three times in the 1920's.

His personal life was a mixture of tragedy and happiness. Sometime in 1914, with the aid of the sisters in her girlhood convent school, his mother overcame the addiction to morphine, and the family life reverted to a kind of normalcy. Jamie, once his mother had given over drugs, stopped drinking, and, rejoicing in her return to health, was content to stay by her side. But the normalcy did not last. James O'Neill, suffering greatly from abdominal cancer, died in 1920. Ella proved to be a capable property manager and with Jamie's help undertook to take care of his estate. In Los Angeles in 1922, she suffered a stroke and died. Jamie immediately returned to the bottle. The night *The Hairy Ape* opened, the train bearing his mother's coffin and his helplessly drunken brother arrived in New York City. O'Neill, again in flight, did not meet the train nor attend the premiere of his play. Jamie died in a sanitarium a year later. In three years, O'Neill's family had been wiped out.

In the same period, however, there were moments of respite when the flight permitted pause. In 1918, O'Neill met and married a young writer, Agnes Boulton, and began to create a family of his own. The two went to live in Provincetown on Cape Cod, where in the dunes, at Peaked Hill Bar some distance from the town, they found an old Coast Guard Station. James O'Neill purchased it as a wedding gift for his son. It was a romantic and lonely place, fringing the sea, an ideal spot for O'Neill to write. Life for a moment seemed balanced and full, especially when Agnes gave birth to O'Neill's second son, Shane Rudraighe.

As his plays became increasingly successful, the two looked for less bohemian, more impressive dwellings, settling first in a large house in Ridgefield, Connecticut, and later, in 1926, in Bermuda where they remodeled a house on Little Turtle Bay called "Spithead." There, their daughter Oona was born in 1925, and the house filled with children and dogs and a stream of visitors. Although he took pleasure in his children, the role of genial host and pater familias did not suit O'Neill. For his work he needed undisturbed solitude. Agnes, however, was more socially inclined, and perhaps inevitably the marriage was increasingly troubled.

During the summer of 1926, while they vacationed at the Belgrade Lakes in Maine, O'Neill met again an actress, Carlotta Monterey, who had appeared as Mildred in *The Hairy Ape*. Carlotta had been born and raised in California. She was partly of Danish origin, but had a Spanish-style beauty on which she capitalized when she went on the stage. She had been educated for a time in England and thrice married. She had tastes and behavior nurtured in a sophisticated world very different from that of Agnes O'Neill. O'Neill's fascination with her poise and his attraction to her beauty soon led to a serious love affair. In 1928, he requested that Agnes divorce him and sailed with Carlotta for Europe.

Restlessly awaiting the divorce, the two moved around France and made a disturbing trip to the Orient. Finally they settled in France at a château near Tours. In 1929, when the divorce was final, they were married, and Carlotta provided him with the strict silence he needed to write. He settled down to important work on a trilogy, *Mourning Becomes Electra*, whose writing would occupy him for the next three years. They returned to the United States in 1931 for its successful production.

Shortly after the opening, they went south to Sea Island, Georgia, and built a palatial home along the water's edge. There, writing more slowly than he had in earlier years, O'Neill labored through eight drafts of *Days Without End*, which, along with an earlier play, *Dynamo*, was conceived as part of a trilogy exploring the need for god in a godless world. The working title of the trilogy was "Myths for the God-forsaken."

Neither play succeeded in production, and as if in rebellion against the theological inquiries, he awoke one morning with the shape of a play clear in his mind. He wrote it rapidly and with joy, and *Ah, Wilderness!*, his "comedy of recollection," became one of his best loved plays. Here he made his first step toward facing the dreaded story of his family's past and the years of his New London boyhood. The play, however, does not face the facts of his early life, but rather surrounds characters reminiscent of his father and mother with a nostalgic glow and loving sentiment. The play has proved to be one of the finest and most enduring American comedies.

During the 1930's, as the Great Depression caused the United States to take stock of its values and to question its traditions, O'Neill felt a responsibility like that of many writers of the time to face the ironic fact that the American, who once could legitimately believe that his country was a bright land of infinite possibility, was now reduced to a shivering, starving inhabitant of a wasteland in which dreams offered no hope. Unlike many of his fellow dramatists who found in political and social causes the possibility of a decent future, O'Neill rejected radical optimism and took a much darker view. He turned to an exploration of first causes and asked why the United States had come to such a deprived condition. He began to plan a dramatic work that would, as he put it, "dig at the roots of the big sickness" of his nation.

The exploration at first took the form of a single play, intended as the third of the God-forsaken trilogy. As the idea germinated, however, the scheme grew to a "play of generations"—a five play Cycle of an American family. Obsessed with the idea, he went further and the Cycle grew until in plan it became an eleven play account of an American family traced from the pre-Revolutionary War period to the 1930's. Its story was encapsulated in its title: *A Tale of Possessors Self-dispossessed.* America, through its greedy attempts to possess and exploit what the land offered freely to all, had in the end dispossessed itself of its rightful heritage. He took his theme from the New Testament: "For what shall it profit a man if he shall gain the whole world, and lose his own soul?"

The writing of the Cycle and of *Ah, Wilderness!* point toward the ending of the seeking flight. In the Cycle, no religious considerations were evident as they had been in the plays that centered on man's necessity to belong to some governing force. Now the history of the American past was turned as a searchlight to permit exploration of the trauma of the present. At the same time, the nostalgic "comedy of recollection" was O'Neill's first attempt to face his own past. History and memory combined to become the twin centers of his creative attention.

The Cycle occupied him for five years, from early 1935 through 1939, but there were times when writing was impossible. He was set upon by continual illness that made him at times a partial invalid. Warned by his doctor that he should put aside creative work for a time, he and Carlotta went to Seattle, Washington, where he hoped to do research on one of the Cycle plays. There, in the fall of 1936, it was announced that he had won the Nobel Prize for Literature, an honor that has yet to come to another American dramatist.[*]

Leaving Seattle in December, the O'Neills travelled south to visit Carlotta's family—her mother and her daughter by an earlier marriage—in Oakland, California. There, in December, O'Neill was stricken with appendicitis. Post-operative complications kept him in the hospital until Spring. During the enforced respite, the couple decided to sell Sea Island and find a home in California.

They found a property in the western hills above the town of Danville, once part of a great Spanish land grant, the Rancho San Ramon. It was an ideal site, remote, sheltered, and peaceful. They purchased 158 acres, and razed an old adobe farmhouse in order to begin construction of their new home which they called "Tao House."

In the study at Tao House, the seeking flight came to an end. There, O'Neill worked arduously on the Cycle, writing notes and scenarios of many thousand words and unproduceably long manuscript drafts of most of the plays. It was cruelly intense work. A change in an early play was sure to bear consequences into the third and fourth generation. Drafts written in O'Neill's tiny handwriting were typed by Carlotta, then revised repeatedly as he went forward in his plan. In the end, the project proved too large, too difficult. His failing health exhausted him, and a tremor made it often impossible to write at all. He completed only one Cycle play, *A Touch of the Poet*. Its unfinished sequel, *More Stately Mansions,* survives in a single-spaced typescript of some 500 pages with manuscript revisions. The rest he destroyed when it became clear that he would not live to finish them.

---

[*] In 1993, a production of *"Anna Christie"* was judged at the Tony awards as the best revival of the year. Although his name was not mentioned at the ceremonies, it may be held that O'Neill has now won a Tony.

Not only illness, but his family also raised problems for his work. Eugene, Jr. had achieved a fine academic record and was teaching Classic Studies at Yale University. Shane, however, was unreceptive to higher education and found no goal toward which he would work with diligence. Oona, left under her mother's care, became a stellar member of New York's Cafe Society and was named the "Number One Debutante" by the public relation flacks of the Stork Club. Later, with a screen career in mind, she went to Hollywood and there met and married Charles Chaplin. Chaplin was her father's age and caught in the eye of a public scandal because of a dubious paternity suit and attacks on his patriotism by the FBI. O'Neill, who had provided for the welfare and education of all his children, renounced Agnes's children bitterly.

One day he also gave up the Cycle. On June 5, 1939, he wrote in his Work Diary, "Decide what I have done on 5th play is n[o] g[ood], so tear it up. Feel fed up and stale on Cycle after four and a half years of not thinking of other work—will do me good to lay on shelf and forget it for a while—do a play which has nothing to do with it." Two days later, he recorded that he had found the new play a "fine title 'The Iceman Cometh.'" With that he circled in on his own past and entered his finest creative period.

By the end of June, he had outlined both *The Iceman Cometh*, the play that cast back to his days at Jimmy-the-Priest's saloon, and *Long Day's Journey into Night*, the re-creation of the lives of his family and himself in Monte Cristo Cottage. Now, he was at last ready to go back into his memories, to face his past and try to understand what it was that had sent him on his flight from his boyhood in Monte Cristo Cottage to Tao House at the other end of the continent. When they were completed, the autobiographical plays proved each in its way to be a masterpiece. *Hughie*, the only completed play of a projected cycle of one-act plays, is a lyric exploration of the attempt of a Broadway race-track tout to find a way to touch another human being—an inarticulate night clerk—so that he will not be left alone with his fears in the pre-dawn hours in the lobby of a cheap New York hotel. Erie, the central figure, speaking what is essentially an hour-long monologue, is modeled on O'Neill's brother, Jamie. Jamie appears again in *A Moon for the Misbegotten,* wherein O'Neill faced at last the death of his mother and the agony of his brother at failing her. As he had done with the protagonist of *Hughie,* in the longer play O'Neill found a way to bring the character for whom Jamie served as model to a kind of salvation—in this work in the arms of a giant, maternal, peasant woman who brings him love and peace and freedom from guilt.

In none of the Tao House plays does a quest for a god enter consideration. At the end of his creative life, O'Neill viewed men and women as so deprived, so naked, so needy that survival was only possible if, groping through the dark, one could find another person to cling to. Such a view of life is not an easy one, yet in the context of the world in which the plays were written they carry a profound truth. To read *The Iceman Cometh* against the background of the great Depression and the Second World War, to consider that it is not a great emotional distance from Harry Hope's saloon to the concentration camps of Nazi Germany, and to see these characters clutching at the straw of a "life-lie," a "hopeless hope," and clinging to one another in order to keep themselves from the chill world of the dead is to experience drama at its most moving and profound. O'Neill's understanding of the down-and-outs he depicted in *The Iceman Cometh* and of his family in *Long Day's Journey into Night* transcends easy pity, offering instead, a full, rich belief in the power of human beings to survive—a concept that is in itself a testament to the value of human nature. His understanding of desperate men and women is something that audiences must share, because in these characters there is a part of all of us and of the universal.

What remains for their creator can be briefly told. The war brought rationing, enisling them in their hillside fastness. Servants on whom they depended in their illnesses were off to war work. Trips to the doctor were difficult. In the end, Tao House which O'Neill once called his "final harbor" had to be sold. In New York City in 1945, O'Neill found strength to oversee rehearsals of *The Iceman Cometh* and *A Moon for the Misbegotten.* The first was received with interest and respect, the second, beset with casting problems, closed out of town. Its failure marked the end of O'Neill's life in the theatre.

The tremor had now become so severe that any writing was painful and often impossible. His family life was unbearable. Shane had become addicted to drugs, and Eugene, Jr. to alcohol. In 1950, Eugene, Jr., after leaving his teaching at Yale University, and failing in his effort to develop a career in radio and television, committed suicide. Their illnesses jeopardizing their marriage, Carlotta and he for a time were alienated from one another, but in the end they were reunited. Before he died he made her his literary executrix. He died on November 27, 1953 and was buried in Forest Hills Cemetery in Boston.

When the flight ended, his reputation was at a low ebb. Three years later, however, a revival of *The Iceman Cometh,* directed by José Quintero and starring Jason Robards, became a sensation in New York City. Shortly thereafter the same team staged *Long Day's Journey into Night,* for which O'Neill posthumously received his fourth Pulitzer Prize. Thereafter, his reputation grew rapidly, surpassing what it had been in the 1920's. This time, however, the playwright was understood to be more than an inventive and exciting writer. He had become a dramatist who spoke not only to the nation, but to the whole world, deserving of universal acclaim.

From the Silence of Tao House

This afternoon, I shall not try to break new ground or to present insights which you, as students of Eugene O'Neill, already possess. What novelty I have to offer comes because as an official of the Eugene O'Neill Foundation at Tao House, I have had opportunity to work for several years in and around his California home. This chance may be called in a small way "unique," and I propose today to speak personally and descriptively of aspects of the house as I have come to sense what it meant to O'Neill.

With your indulgence, I shall begin by narrating an episode that I hope will not be so personal as to seem irrelevant to your concerns. It was my first real contact with Tao House as a building in which O'Neill lived and wrote, and it remains at the core of my sentiments about the house. Oddly, though, the experience had little to do with him.

Three years ago now, in December, I was waiting with the president of the Foundation for an official visitation from several persons connected with the Department of the Interior from Washington. The meeting had been set for three in the afternoon, but the visitors, driving in from a distance were late, and, as it turned out, lost. It was a miserable day. A storm was blowing down the valley from the north end of San Francisco Bay, and the house and grounds darkened rapidly. The weather was a problem because the Foundation had only recently assumed responsibility for the property and had been unable as yet to provide even the barest amenities. The propane tanks to fuel the furnace were empty; there were one or two low wattage bulbs burning

A paper read to a meeting of the Modern Language Association in New York City, Friday, Dec. 29, 1978

dimly in fixtures in a few of the rooms; and three folding chairs were set existentially in the large living room. There was no other furniture. The house was gaunt, empty and featureless.

I built a fire in the living room fireplace and so procured a little light and heat, but from that center, the house faded away into shadow. A message came: our visitors had arrived at a remote spot in the valley and would appreciate transport. Car space being at a premium, I waited at the house while the Foundation president went to find the travellers. It was by now nearly night. The storm was close. Upon leaving, the president laughed at me, crouched in a huddle before the fire and said "Now you'll have a chance to find out if the house is haunted." As the door closed, the rain came slanting against the window panes like knives.

There, alone for an hour, I walked the corridors of Tao House in the dark, trying to feel its quality. It was not haunted. Whatever ghosts there were—the ghosts of the four haunted Tyrones—had left the house when its master did. What I found is hard to describe—an extraordinary silence for one thing, and I felt a sense of protection, as if the house were a caretaker, guarding my well-being, and in so doing, recovering its function.

I do not mean to cause embarrassment by anthropomorphizing a structure of brick and tile, but what I felt that night was real as fantasy can sometimes hold a truth. I could not find O'Neill, although I tried to project myself into his essence as I walked where he had. The house alone linked us, protecting me as it had once protected him. Mark you, it was more than a question of shelter or dryness or warmth. The sense I had was of something more active, more participant in the life process, more—the word is ridiculous—concerned.

What I am trying to convey is not easy to make real, but what it amounts to is that Tao House is a special place. O'Neill applied several casual complimentary epithets to it: "my final harbor," "Carlotta's masterpiece," and the like. As with the château at Le Plessis, where O'Neill and Carlotta lived prior to their marriage, Tao House, heard of but not seen, carries an aura of grandeur with its name. But the château, we have learned, was a little tacky, and certainly Tao House is by no means an elaborate or stately mansion. It is a graceful house, but it is also efficient, and one that, for all its square footage, is not oversize. The plan is clean and simple, as is the structure. There are few stud walls. The exterior and most of the interior walls are built of basalite bricks piled in the manner of adobe construction. A double course of the bricks forms the outside walls and those enclosing the large garden, making the exterior surfaces sixteen inches thick. Painted, they seem like whitewashed adobe and form a striking contrast to the black tiles on the long roof.

When O'Neill lived in the house, both the exterior and interior walls were flat white. Inside, they contrasted with the rich, dark blue of the ceiling (eight coats, until the painter finally achieved Carlotta's desired color) and the red-brown floor made of massive tiles laid in a random pattern. The doors were red, painted to emulate Chinese lacquerwork. O'Neill's bedroom and study are less striking. The walls of his bedroom are a soft gray, and the study is paneled and painted with a technique called "antiquing." Between the ceiling beams the Chinese red motif re-appears.

Despite the white walls and the vivid, contrasting colors, it is a dark house. In the living room, the double-hung windows are large, but they are set far apart, in the corners of the room. The drenching light of summer was excluded, just as the rain and cold were that December night. There were no drapes, only Venetian blinds, and as light entered it was reflected into the central areas of the room from large, dark blue mirrors. No light fixtures were placed on the walls and the sense one still has is of living under water, in a subaqueous world where light seems part of the silence.

The effect of enforced chiaroscuro is changed somewhat when one recognizes that, the living room aside, all the main rooms, bedrooms and study have a means of emerging immediately into the out-of-doors—into the walled garden, or to the east onto a broad terrace, or to a choice of upper galleries and balconies. The house is a little like a cave in its protective qualities, but it is also cave-like in its uninhibited, direct opening into the air and a world of great natural beauty.

Outside Tao House, the hills rise steeply to the west and give on a wilderness area, forested with pine, manzanita and madrone. Bobcats, coyotes and deer move through the land, and a mated pair of blue herons nests near the reservoir. Abundant springs provide water for the house, livestock and swimming pool even in years of drought, and immediately around the house lie orchards of almonds and walnuts and oranges, fringed with redwoods and tall pines. Tao House (O'Neill, after the fashion of the day, called it "Tay-o House") lies about thirty-five miles from San Francisco, overlooking the small San Ramon Valley. Before the O'Neills built, there was an adobe farmhouse on the land, an outriders' hostel for a Spanish land grant, the Pacheco Rancho. An old barn on the property dates from that earlier time. From below, the site is not so commanding as that of many neighboring homes. Tao House rests in a cup of hills, folded in by east-running ridges and arroyos that descend from the summit of the Las Trampas Ridge, and is hidden from sight of all but a few locations on the valley floor. However, from the site itself there is no mote in the outlook. To the east, a broad panorama of the valley's orchards and the heavy-shouldered mass of Mount Diablo compel attention so that there is no feeling of its being limited or shut in. The house was perhaps a harbor, but it was not a prison or a sanatorium. It was a caretaker, not a jailer.

O'Neill's need to find caretakers throughout his life has been well documented. In *Long Day's Journey into Night,* O'Neill has Mary Tyrone, the name given in the play to his mother, say to him:

O, I'm sure you don't feel half as badly as you make out.
You're such a baby. You like to get us worried so we'll make

a fuss over you.... I'm only teasing, dear. I know how miserably uncomfortable you must be. But you feel better today, don't you?... All the same, you've grown much too thin. You need to rest all you can. Sit down and I'll make you comfortable. *(He sits down in the rocking chair and she puts a pillow behind his back.)* There. How's that?...All you need is your mother to nurse you. Big as you are, you're still the baby of the family to me, you know.

That her son responds to such attention eagerly is attested by his bitter, broken words toward the end of the play: "All this talk about loving me—and you won't even listen when I try to tell you how sick—" But his mother cuts off his words, denies her care, and precipitates tragedy.

In his biography of O'Neill, Louis Sheaffer has shown how important in O'Neill's life was the early "substitute mother," the nurse Sarah Sandy, on whom the young O'Neill came to rely with a dependence that was tantamount to devotion. Without his father to play the role that O'Neill envisioned in the character of Nat Miller in *Ah, Wilderness,* he turned to his brother for adolescent initiation into sexual realities. But nurse and brother were only the first in a long line. There was his Greenwich Village friend, Terry Carlin, his first producer, George Cram Cook, the critic, Kenneth Macgowan, his editor, Saxe Commins and Lawrence Langner, the Theatre Guild producer. And there was the ultimate caretaker, Carlotta Monterey.

O'Neill's relationship to these people was different in quality from the relations normally developed between writer and producer or editor or even wife. Without more certain information, the reason O'Neill and Agnes separated can only be surmised. Possibly her nature demanded a freedom of mind and action that made it impossible for her to become one of the special guardians. Carlotta, on the other hand, found a life of caring devotion sufficient. She was content with what O'Neill in an early play, *Servitude,* called "Pan in Logos."

In 1958, Carlotta said to me, "He came to me and asked me to serve him tea. 'Tea?' I thought, knowing all about his drinking, 'That man wants tea?' But I served him tea, and he drank it, and he came again several more times, and one day he said to me, 'Carlotta, I need you,' and I thought, 'Oh, oh. Here it comes!' But he said 'I've been making some money and people know me, and I have to live respectably, and I don't know how. I need someone to plan the meals and put guest towels in the bathroom and....'"

Her speech continued perhaps more rehearsed than improvised. She bought him clothes, taught him the rudiments of gracious living, introduced him to life in European watering holes, and, as his habits of writing became clear to her, she built him walls and created houses that could aid in the caretaking responsibilities.

The first caretaker house was created in France as Carlotta reshaped the château at Le Plessis, providing in one of its tourelles a cell where O'Neill could work undisturbed by any intrusion. There the work became the central preoccupation of their lives. A second attempt was on Sea Island in Georgia where she built Casa Genotta, a name coined by a portmanteau compression of their two first names. The house was beautiful and served well, but the climate and the noise from the neighboring estates made it less than satisfactory. And so at last by a series of coincidences they came to Oakland, California, where Carlotta's family lived. In time, she created Tao House.

How influential Tao House was on his writing can only be guessed. One or two things at least are not fanciful. In the scene in the walled garden of *More Stately Mansions,* O'Neill requires a summer house with a doorway painted a Chinese lacquer red, the color he had seen on the doors of his home. In the play, the summer house, placed trimly in the walled garden, is not unlike the small box room in the Tao House garden which nestles against the high garden wall and is approached by small neat paths, as is required in the play. One thinks as well of the mirrors that continually appear in the Cycle plays: Con Melody's tavern mirror before which he postures in shoddy magnificence and the large mirror in Simon Harford's office before which Simon and Sara make love. As in the tavern and the office, the mirrors of Tao House reflected the life lived there. Before he came to California, O'Neill wrote that life is a solitary cell whose walls are mirrors. To a degree, Tao House realized that image.

There are other things, less definite. Looking from the window in O'Neill's study, one's gaze descends to a "fruited plain," backed by a "purple mountain's majesty." There is something epic about the outlook, as if from that vantage point, the valley was a microcosm of the westering nation whose story O'Neill had set himself to tell in the Cycle. And there was the light—intense brightness that did not penetrate the dim world, exactly as called for in the saloon in *The Iceman Cometh* where the shadows give rise to the image of the "bottom-of-the-sea Rathskellar." And a final instance: The Oregon Shakespeare Festival brought its production of *A Moon for the Misbegotten* to play at Tao House. Without a theatre, the play was staged against a side of the ramshackle barn. Under a full moon, the play seemed to be placed poetically *in situ.*

But Tao House as inspiration was less important than Tao House as caretaker. Under Carlotta's ministrations, the building became the perfect housing for the enormous energy generated in the study. O'Neill's undertaking and accomplishments were prodigious and when illness stopped the writing, the house that had so supported the artist could no longer sustain the man. The war made havoc of services. Tao House is a long way from markets and beyond reach of public transportation. Forced by gasoline rationing to rely on the kindness of strangers, the O'Neills learned to value the people in the town of Danville. Carlotta tried to keep the house going without the one or two servants necessary to maintain the establishment, but she was ill and the duties weighed on her. Their man-of-all-work, Herbert Freeman, departed for war work and left them in an isolation which might have been tolerable were it not for their ill health. But O'Neill was frighteningly sick, and the illness spelled the end, after less than a decade, of the caretaker house.

O'Neill required constant care. A nurse, Kathryne Radovan, was on continual call, but much of his care was left to Carlotta who kept extensive, detailed accounts of his day-to-day condition for the doctor's benefit:

August 6th— feels so low has coffee at 5:30 AM

August 7th— has three doses stramonium of twenty drops each tremor bad in AM but better after third dose. Has less tension in solar plexus after luncheon and dinner. Doesn't sleep

August 8th— three doses stramonium of twenty drops each—complains of "inner" tension—about 3:30 PM has crack-up tremor ghastly—weeping

August 10th— quieter—less strained—eyes losing their 'shine' swims— takes 1 teaspoonful of Duke's Mixture at 6:30 PM and 2 teaspoonful at 2 AM

August 16th— wakes coughing and spits up blood—seems very worried about this—is not well—tremor bad

August 22nd— Gene's cough better; he gets up for about four hours—puts on Hitchcock's belt as his back is bothering him again—belt is painful, rubbing against his vertebrae—eats well—takes Seconal and has a fairly good night

August 23rd— Tapering off Feiler's Mixture also the barbiturates and cough medicines—is nervous, weak, shaky and low mentally. Gave him paraldehyde (two teaspoonful in orange juice with cracked ice) on settling for the night. At long last he goes to sleep but wakes in two hours—nervous—on the

verge of cracking. Make him coffee at 5 AM—his intestines
are bothering him.

It is a dreary and discouraging story. The doctor's record notes
without irony that there is the characteristic "masking" of the face associated with Parkinson's disease, and that he has lost weight, down to 138
pounds, and that while he is not in a critical condition, it would be well
for him to enter a hospital, but that he hates the thought of doing so.

Clearly, the gentle benefits of the remote Tao House could no
longer help either of the O'Neills. The war and the demands of his illness cut the life support systems of the house. Other kinds of caretakers were needed—Carlotta above all, and doctors—the only strangers
and friends who could intrude into the silenced world.

But there were always caretakers. A draft of a letter written by
one of his Oakland doctors requesting a consultation and reviewing
O'Neill's medical history ends with these words:

His wife is resplendent and has been a revelation to me. A beautiful
girl with a brain. Mr. O'Neill is greatly worried at times, but is marvelously
understanding and tolerant. I so much want to be of real help to him.

Scratched out, presumably because it departed from strict
medical propriety, was another sentence:

Mr O'Neill is my notion of a latter-day knight—so patient and kind.
He will be my chief concern as long as he is content with me.

There were always the caretakers.

men and women to "belong" to some center that will free them from
the conflict of forces that beset them.

He expressed the need and its ultimate satisfaction in his birthday poem to Carlotta O'Neill in 1940, a poem he called "Quiet Song in
a Time of Chaos":

> Here
> Is home.
> Is peace.
> Is quiet.
>
> Here
> Is love
> That sits by the hearth
> And smiles into the fire,
> As into a memory
> Of happiness,
> As into the eyes
> Of quiet.
>
> Here
> Is faith
> That can be silent.
> It is not afraid of silence.
> It knows happiness
> Is a deep pool
> Of quiet.
> ...
> Here?
> Where is here ?
> But you understand.
> In my heart

Within your heart
Is home.
Is peace.
Is quiet.

It was Carlotta who brought him the satisfaction he describes and which he found finally at the home she made for him at Tao House across San Francisco Bay in the hills above Danville.

Before that time the restless peregrinations continued. With Agnes, his second wife, he found little of what he sought. He wrote her in April, 1927, that he felt their Bermuda house to be *"Our Home!"* (Italics, caps, exclamation point), and he continued to assert his feeling that "this place is in some strange symbolical fashion our reward, that it is the permanent seat of our family—like some old English family estate.... The thought of the place is indissolubly intermingled with my love for you, with our nine years of marriage that, after much struggle, have finally won to this haven, this ultimate island where we may rest and live toward our dreams with a sense of permanence and security that here we do belong."

But Agnes, busily raising two young children, interested in socializing, trying to compete somewhat with her husband as a writer, did not respond to his creative necessities, and by the year's end, he had asked her for a divorce and was preparing to leave for Europe with Carlotta Monterey.

What he sought in a home was a protected world which would provide the sealed-off space he needed in order to create. He was an obsessive writer. When he was living in an abandoned Coast Guard station on Cape Cod, a teacher from a local girls' academy with her class in tow arrived unexpectedly across the sand dunes to ask him to write a play for their dramatic study. When they had gone, he vowed that he would someday build a home that had a high wall all around it and a brace of the fiercest Irish wolfhounds to patrol the wall on both sides.

Carlotta, who must have known how to cope with domestic loneliness, built the home he needed. Her first try was at a château in France and then, when they had married and returned to the United States, she created a house in Georgia which they named after themselves: Casa Genotta.

Neither was fully satisfactory, and finally they came to California to settle near San Francisco. Up in Marin County they felt it was too rainy; on the Peninsula it was too full of socialites, or so they said. But when they discovered the acreage below the Las Trampas ridge in the San Ramon Valley, it seemed to be paradise.

Tao House was Carlotta's creation from first to last, and there in 1937, the two entered into a peaceable kingdom. There, finally, with Carlotta as the grenadier at the gate, O'Neill was free of all intrusion, and he set to work on the two major occupations of his maturity, the eleven-play historical Cycle, *A Tale of Possessors Self-dispossessed*, and the autobiographical plays, *Long Day's Journey into Night, A Moon for the Misbegotten, Hughie,* and *The Iceman Cometh.*

He was not to finish the Cycle. Only *A Touch of the Poet* and the unrevised draft of its amazing sequel, *More Stately Mansions*, remain. But in the autobiographical plays, the plays he lived to write, he was able to turn back to the past—to the days at Monte Cristo Cottage and to the memory of his tortured mother, father and brother in the lean-to room—to "face his dead," and to come to an understanding of what had caused his lifelong flight.

The consequence of that understanding is the reason for celebrating his memory. To read O'Neill is to see him only obscurely through a dark glass. His fifty completed plays, now published in the new edition by the Library of America, are probably not to be called great "literature," but they are great "theatre," a very different thing. Read Shakespeare for his poetry; read Shaw for his witty rhetoric—yet when Shakespeare and Shaw move onstage, language loses its pre-eminence and is submerged in that movement a drama makes where literature cannot go—physically through real space and real time, pulling the audience toward an experience entirely different from that to be had by reading. O'Neill's poetry and his rhetoric is peculiarly of the theatre, at one with his use of shadow and light, soliloquy and monologue, music and silence. With him, the dramatic experience is nearly all.

But it is a special experience. Why are actors eager to play O'Neill? Because he asks for their best and rewards them when he gets it. As the careers of many American actors, notably Jason Robards and Colleen Dewhurst, demonstrate, they are great roles and they lead to greatness in the performer.

Why do audiences come—sometimes grumbling at the sorrows to which they are to be exposed and the length of time of the exposure? Almost always, they are surprised at how deeply they are moved, and it is interesting that often they are as responsive to the playwright who has done this to them as to the play. In the delighted buzz of conversation that filled the lobby when the audience left *Marco Millions,* one heard the name "O'Neill," bursting like a bubble over all other conversational sounds.

Audiences find that there is variety: simple, affectionate realism as in the early sea plays, satire mingled with sophisticated fantasy, as in *Marco Millions,* the warmest human comedy as in *Ah, Wilderness!* contrasting with tragic heartbreak in *Long Day's Journey into Night,* or blended brilliantly in the same play, as in *A Moon for the Misbegotten,* psychological probing of an unusually intense kind, as in *Desire Under the Elms, Strange Interlude* and *Mourning Becomes Electra,* theatrical excitements such as the experience of the drums in *The Emperor Jones,* and philosophical plays like *The Iceman Cometh* which introduced the American theatre to the world of existentialism some years before the philosophers found the term.

Above all, they are convinced by the truth of O'Neill's understanding of his own desperate need to belong, of his toleration for human failure, of the power of his pity for the lonely and the lost. As all writers must do if they are to be remembered past their moment, O'Neill convinces us that his truth is our truth, and that his understanding has contributed to our own. Is it too much to say that in reminding us of our humanity, O'Neill makes us more human?

Tao House stands at the opposite end of a long journey from Monte Cristo Cottage. More than a continent stands between them. A lifetime of creative work that was meditative, startling, courageous and, for the American theatre, formative, lies between the two houses. O'Neill's daring imagination led our theatre away from the trivial romanticism of *Monte Cristo* into the modern world, and much that he pioneered is still being done by younger men who follow in his footsteps without filling his shoes.

They buried a time capsule out at Tao House the other day. I suspect that when it is exhumed a hundred years from today O'Neill's voice will still be heard in the theatre he in large part created.

But to return and conclude: Tao House was a demi-Paradise, but like all Edens, it could not last. The strictures of the war isolated them in the Las Trampas hills, and illness crippled him so that he could no longer write. The great works yet to come were sealed within him and he became their living tomb. Again he was forced on the move—to a New York apartment, a house on Marblehead Neck in Massachusetts, and finally to the Hotel Shelton in Boston.

He was ever alert to the ironies of fate: his last recorded words were: "I knew it! I knew it! Born in a goddam hotel room and goddamit, dying in a hotel room!"

But we should be thankful that there came a time when he found a true home in California, one which played its substantial part in enabling him to create the major works of the twentieth century American theatre.

Mrs. O'Neill once said to me "You must never use the word 'happiness' in speaking of O'Neill!" But I think both the O'Neills might forgive us if once in a hundred years we wish him "Happy Birthday."

O'Neill In Love

E
ugene O'Neill in love." The phrase seems almost self-contradic-
tory. With the exception of his two romantic comedies, *"Anna
Christie"* and *Ah, Wilderness!,* love as it was commonly presented in America drama does not surface in O'Neill's plays. Fatal passion
there is in plenty; couples welded in a bondage of love and hate are almost too frequent; universal love like that of Lazarus for all mankind,
and ignorance of love as in the character of Marco Polo are given stage
space; but the cheerful happy ending of many twentieth century dramas and films is one O'Neill avoided with studied concern. Even when
he approached romance, he was circumspect. Anna Christie is allowed
to have her man, but the happy ending is smothered in foreboding of
darkness to come. Richard Miller in *Ah, Wilderness!* is allowed to kiss
his girl, but the last image of him standing in the moonlight "like a statue of Love's Young Dream" is nostalgic and has little to do with the
world of reality.

Yet in his private life, quite separate from his writing, O'Neill
was a man capable of intense passion, deep love and staunch fidelity
once he was assured that his faith had found an answering truth. In his
early life there were many casual sexual encounters. These were of little
moment and go unrecorded except as they may be reflected in the
plays—the second act of *Welded,* for example, or Jamie's excoriation of
the "fascinating vampires" toward the end of *Long Day's Journey into
Night.* His correspondence, however, tells of love affairs far from casual or transient, and which, taken together, add to a committed search
for love and fidelity.

*Read on Valentine's Day, 1984, to the Rossmore Auxiliary of the Eugene O'Neill
Foundation, Tao House*

There were seven women who were important to him at various stages in his life, from adolescence to a time when old and sick and frustrated he caught sight of a freshness and a youth he knew was no longer possible for him to have.

The first was a girl named Marion Welch who lived in Hartford, Connecticut but who visited in the summer in New London, the only place O'Neill could have called a "home town." The romance began in the summer of 1905, when O'Neill was sixteen. Like many a teenage romance in that far-gone time, it was more theoretical than passionate. O'Neill taught her to row, and they took snapshots of one another. The snapshots exist—amateur kodakery at its worst, double-exposed, tilted, light-struck, showing the two at various summer moments. One shows Eugene lolling in the stern of a rowboat while, presumably, his pupil plied the oars. Only one of the collection is worth attention. It shows a short, cluttered stretch of deserted beach fenced in by two stone walls, and backed by trees along a street. A rowboat is pulled above the waterline, and farther down the street are houses. It is a worthless snapshot of unimpressive property, but perhaps in the moonlight, the little strip of sand gained some of the enchantment O'Neill cast over the small beach front in the fourth act of *Ah, Wilderness!* where Richard Miller, who was the same age as Eugene when he wrote to Marion, made his peace with Muriel McComber.

O'Neill's romance with Marion lacked the sentiment of that between Richard and Muriel. It was not until she returned to Hartford and he was safely out of the path of temptation, that the romance began in something like earnest. O'Neill, it appears, was studying French, and in his lessons he found a name for her that was not without charm: "Boutade," which means "whim" or "caprice."

The correspondence begins with a small effusion of adolescent love-longing:

325 Pequot Ave.
New London, Conn.

Ma Chère "Boutade,"

You cannot imagine with what feeling of joy I received your letter this morning. All the more so, because it was unexpected, for I thought that, by this time, New London and all in it were but faint memories of the misty past to you. I am very happy to find out I was mistaken.

I cannot say how much I missed and still miss you. New London has now relapsed into a somnambulant state which is far from pleasing and all on account of your departure....

I miss your "windmill motion" in the row boat but, to be truthful, it was far from a windmill towards the end and more like an expert's. (Now will you be good). I have not even been up to hear the orchestra at the Pequot for fear I should be overcome by pleasant memories (and the bum music).

Those pictures are exceedingly unkind to me and I hope I do not look anything like them. They are good however considering the sun was in our faces (and the subjects as you cruelly mentioned). Do not forget to send me the others and if I may ask for the millionth time for your photo "Please! Ah! Please! I think you're the meanest girl I ever knew." But all joking aside I assure you that I want it ever so much. And let us keep up this correspondence, begun with such "earnest of success" If you knew what a break it is in the dull, monotonous existence up here I feel sure you would not refuse.

I am getting to be a perfect bookworm and read all morning, swim in the afternoon as usual...and read all night. Can you beat it ?...

Well, the sand in my hour glass is about run out and I must "put on the brakes." Please send me your photo with the other pictures and thus make me even more than I am now.

Your eternal slave.
Eugene O'Neill

In August she sent him snapshots but not the coveted photograph of herself. He calls her remembrance a "half give-in" but suggests she return to New London to continue her rowing lessons. He praises her for having learned by heart Poe's "Annabel Lee" and continues:

> Some of the lines express my feelings exactly especially in the following:
>> "And neither the angels in heaven
>> Nor the demons down under the sea
>> Can ever dissever my soul from the soul
>> Of beautiful Annabel Lee."
>
> Except her name is not Annabel Lee but M...W.... But what is it you said one time about personal remarks?

Unskilled at wooing, he seeks safety in literature. Marion, surprisingly was reading Darwin. Eugene rejected her choice and unexpectedly recommended that she read Dumas:

> I don't see how anyone can go to Darwin for enjoyment. Alex. Dumas père pour le mien. I could read every book in the world and no heroes could ever replace "D'Artagnan, Athos, Porthos and Aramis," "Monte Cristo" and "Bussy" in my estimation.

Evidently *Monte Cristo* still held a vestigial charm for the actor's son, as did *Macbeth*. O'Neill had memorized it on a bet with his father and the letters are larded with short quotations from the play.

The letters continue in the same flirtatious vein. She won't send the photograph ("Please! Ah! Ple...ease!"). He and his brother go on the river together:

> The other night it was clear and the moon was full (but I wasn't!) but the wind was blowing a gale and the sea was pretty high and "mon frère et moi" went out in the boat and rowed way out in the Sound. It was fine. The waves were so high that when we were on top of them we could see the mortgages on the houses in Shelter Island....

Do write and throw a little sunlight into the chasm of Despair where lies
Your devoted slave
Eugene

The summer of 1905, to hear him tell it, dragged along. He had a small thrill:

I met an agent for the Madison Automobile Co. and he has a 60 horse power machine worth seven thousand in which he has taken me out. We went to Norwich and back (29 miles) in forty minutes. I have not been able to part my hair since, I was so frightened....

Well I guess I have "snowballed my layout" of interesting things to relate and so "Au revoir ma chérie je vous aimerai toujours et je vous baisserai en pensée."
Your devoted admirer
Eugene.

Love, evidently, was easier in beginning French which not only made the declaration of passion seem sexier, but also put it into a discreet code suitable for chaste ears and guardian parents. However, there was perhaps another problem that rendered the adolescent flirtatiousness hollow. He continued to write her from his preparatory school, Betts Academy, and spoke of occasional trips to New York City with his brother and older friends. According to Louis Sheaffer it was in this period when his brother took Eugene to a brothel and the boy's traumatic sexual initiation took place. There is no hint of the episode in the letters to Boutade which continue with accounts of shows seen in New York City, football games, and school pranks, but clearly as he went on to other pursuits and readied himself for entry into Princeton, puppy-love and letter writing flagged. The last extant letter written in December, 1905, is addressed somewhat formally:

My dear Marion—

It is, I suppose, useless to ask for pardon for making you wait such a long time for an answer to your letter. All I have to say is that it got here just before our Thanksgiving vacation and I forgot it in the excitement of going to New York. I just happened to find it today in my desk and determined "to do the deed before the purpose cooled" and write you immediately. I hope I am forgiven, for I cherish the remembrance of some of the happiest days of my life (passed in a rowboat in New London harbor) far too greatly to have any hitch come in our correspondence. I also have a picture of a certain girl with a dog (Teddy?) which I cherish even if it is only a half give-in.)

The balance of the letter concerns reading recommendations and his disdain for his father's play, "old worm eaten 'Monte Cristo.'" The substance of the letter having dwindled away, he concludes with *Macbeth* and minimal French:

The "bell invites me" to go to class so "au revoir."
Your own
Eugene

Even the French has lost its charm and "Boutade" fades into memory to be recalled with affection as Muriel McComber in the scene in the rowboat beached in the harbor in *Ah, Wilderness!*

O'Neill's next recorded romance came nine years later in 1914, when, after an abortive year at Princeton and a picaresque and somewhat degenerate life at sea and in the New York slums, he returned to respectability, to New London, and to his education, this time at Harvard as a student of George Pierce Baker's class in playwriting.

The girl was the beautiful Beatrice Ashe, tall, dark-haired and, in her photographs, unpretentiously exotic. She lived in New London, and he courted her assiduously, though, one suspects, with ultimate chasteness. He wrote her poems, "Full Many a Cup" and "On Our Beach," commemorating times spent with her, and in July, 1914:

> Oh Bea, Bea, Bea, I sure am longing for you at this moment. I want to find My Place once more and rest my weary sunburnt head and briny hair. I'd like awful much to just give you an inkling of what you mean to me, of how I have become one great aching desire—but I can't now. Someday I'm going to gather all my boo-ful words together and make the effort. For the present you'll have to read "Full Many a Cup" over again. It's the nearest I've come so far.
>
> I hope you're writing too. Your "I Love you" is near my heart.
>
> Good night, Dear Blessed Damozel, and a long kiss.

Evidently, since "Boutade," the temperature has risen, helped by baby talk (O'Neill was twenty-six, but the year was 1914) and the poetry of Dante Gabriel Rossetti.

Away from her, he remembers some of the minor matters major to lovers and indulges in a little sexual strutting:

> I hope you have not forgotten our picnic—also that you have found no other to carry you across the ford—and that no alien presence has desecrated our beach. I have purchased a brand new one-piece bathing suit in New Haven for use on our strip of sand when we go picnicing. I am simply boo-ful in it. It leaves but little to the inquisitive imagination. I shall have to be put off the regular beach just once for the preservation of my rep. for shamelessness and moral imbecility.

French and literary tidbits were still useful to enchant:

> You know what all my poor letters are: Just feeble attempts to express the great love of you which thrills my soul, the sweet wine of love of you which brims over the chalice of my heart.

By the way I've learned the words of our song—(and from another hussy's sheet of music!)

"Moi, pour deux mots, ces mots d'amour,

Je donnerai bien mes nuits, mes jours,

T'entender dans ce moment suprême

Murmurer tout bas, tout bas, je t'aime!"

That's near it anyway. She sang it to me—and I dreamed of you—and she dreamed of another absent one—and there you are! "Life is a tragic folly" as Symons remarks—or to be high-brow and quote Browning "Never the time and the place and the loved one altogether." But my Beatrice and I are going to prove him a liar—some day—aren't we, My Own.

Photographs were also part of his wooing. A fellow student in his boarding house took some pictures of him which he offered to send her. In two of them he costumed himself as poetically as his wardrobe would allow; in the others he was all but nude:

Two at my table writing—(soft shirt, Windsor tie, all the properties)—and two in a—well how shall I say it?—well, in nothing but what the Indians used to wear—not feathers, silly!—around their loins. The artist wanted them for help in his studies of the nude. (I am now a model, wot?)

Shall I send you all of them if you are good? There's really nothing immodest about the nude ones, you know—not nearly so much as my one-piece suit ones. I run the risk of losing your love by this offer. You may take one flash at me, unadorned—and say "So this is what they give green certificates with! Take it away!"

Before him, dimly, a lifetime as a playwright began to take form.

My dearest dear, if you could see the obstacles in the path of the prospective playwright as I have seen them today I'm afraid you'd feel like a soldier in the forlorn hope. Many a severe jolt of discouragement awaits you down the long trail. Your love will be put to tests such as few loves are ever put to but *please, please* do stick for I have faith in the ultimate outcome, and without you—Oh the thought is too unbearable! Your love is my whole life....

Dear! Dear! thrice dear one! How can I whisper, my lips against your heart, the love I feel, the passion of my longing for you? .... Now I can only hold up a faded stocking and kiss it—so!—cuddle a dilapidated red bathing cap and kiss it—so!—press your three pictures to my heart and kiss them—so! so! so!

From Cambridge, he details his life at Harvard and provides glimpses into his developing skill as a playwright, but always to Beatrice he is impassioned, tender, half-humorous, as if he were acting a role in a romantic melodrama:

I have just had a horrible thought and I must sit down and get it off my mind before I forget it. It came to me as I was dreaming on your picture a few minutes ago that you had threatened to take down that confidant of all our joys and sorrows, our kisses and quarrels, that most hallowed of all spots—the hammock. I beg, I implore, I adjure in the name of our love, and the continued hot weather to let it remain. Spare it for the night of my birthday, at least. What if it be cold? We possess a sovereign remedy for all low temperatures—each other's arms—do we not?

Letter writing became time-consuming. She asked him not to write so often, and he imposed a one-letter-a-week restriction on the correspondence, a restriction he immediately ignored. They quarreled, but he brushed the quarreling aside as "the explosions of a too-great, stored-up longing, of a need of you which makes life colorless without you. I want you so I fight even you, when you join the opposition." The fetishism continued ("I have kissed all my trophies of you many, many times. It is a solace to me in my solitary hours."), and he again writes her once a day.

"Two at my table writing—(soft shirt, Windsor tie, all the properties)—and two in a—well how shall I say it?—well, in nothing but what the Indians used to wear—not feathers, silly!—around their loins. The artist wanted them for help in his studies of the nude. (I am now a model, wot?)..."

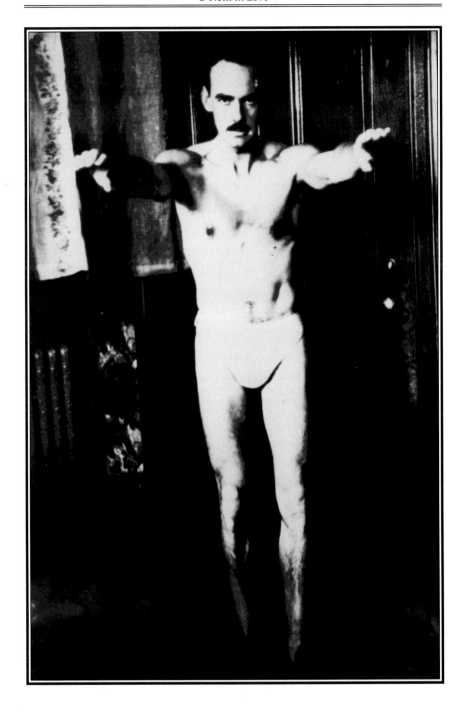

Beatrice's reactions to his ardors can be judged from some of his protestations. After all, the twentieth century had barely started, the town was small and unsophisticated, and a girl's reputation could be damaged severely by association with such a rounder as O'Neill had been. She wrote him suggesting some restraints to his passion. He replied:

As for loving you with a needing love, you must know that it is my great selfish need of you which ever stands foremost in my thoughts. I need you as my goal, my encouragement, my ambition, my end in life. I need your help to become what I want to become. Comrade and Wife, over the smooth road and the flinty trail, hand in hand, bearing our burden, sharing one happiness; under the same star, conquering or crushed by the same fate—that is it!...

Of course I *want* you too. What a poor gray shade I would be if I didn't! The touch of your soft skin, your kisses, your hair, all your loveliness has the power to send a shivering flame through my brain. My blood seethes and fumes, and at times I have forgotten—promises and all weary things, like the rabid immoralist I am. One cannot dam a river without letting some of it flow over. And my passion flows as fiercely toward you as any smoking rapids. I assert it! I am proud of it! Soul without body is as crippled as body without soul. Let us be proud also of our passion! Let it be frank and open, therefore innocent. Only what hides and hangs its head is guilty. Sin exists only in the consciousness of sinning. Evil is—where you see it!

Pardon this ethical philosophizing but you must understand the inherent innocence of my "I want yous." To mistake it for lust would be doing me an injustice. It is part of my love for you and is as strong and free from a sense of guilt as the love of my soul for yours.

The "ethical philosophizing" did not entirely convince Beatrice, although she answered his letters and welcomed him when he came back to New London on short visits.

By December, the letters had assumed, along with the passionate rhetoric, a proprietary tone. He began to address her as "My Own Little Wife" and demanded an unspecified help from her: "Please love me and help me for I need your love and help so much." She tried to apply the brakes to the full course of O'Neill's passion. Through December and on into the Spring of 1915, he wrote her with the same intensity, but she, judging from his reactions to her letters, pulled back a little. She tried to reason with him and got in return: "You are seeking to analyze love, and love is an emotion which will not stand analysis....I don't understand why you say you do not *feel* my love—I *feel* it, my love for you (though I have every reason to doubt yours for me after the past four or five letters).... And 'My Dear Little Wife' makes you skeptical? By all the popes, past, present and future, I swear I wouldn't put down a syllable of it I didn't feel.... *I* don't want you for a friend. All or nothing!"

The letters to Beatrice enlarged and set the style of his wooing and his conception of what love meant from that which he had begun to define as he wrote Marion Welch. He relied heavily on poetic quotation, his own and that of others; he indulged in mild sexual innuendo and some phallic braggadocio; and he set great store on photographs and souvenirs of the beloved with which he indulged in harmless fetishism. He saw the relationship as essentially passionate, but underlying the passion, he revealed his need both to possess the beloved wholly and to depend on her as his "goal, encouragement, ambition and end." Together they would be "conquered or crushed by the same fate." Later, when he attempted to dramatize the concept in two unsuccessful plays, *The First Man* and *Welded,* he thought of the man and woman becoming one being, the woman's personality merging entirely into the man's desire. That Beatrice or any other woman would be unwilling to commit herself completely to such a romantic demand is not hard to understand. In the course of one letter, he hit unwittingly on the truth, writing "Perhaps you think the path ahead with me is too rough?"

Of course she did. She was twenty, he six years older. The simple truth was that his ardors frightened her, and she settled for a smoother path and a calmer existence. The last letter, written after a gap of over a year, is dated July 25, 1916. It is a letter of friendly advice concerning her plans to break away and go to New York to seek a career as an artist. He concluded the letters with a flare-up of the old rhetoric that is as much courteous as passionate ("I love you, I want you, I need you so!") but as a postscript he included some lines from Carl Sandburg's poem "Choices:"

> I come with:
>> salt and bread
>> a terrible job of work
>> and tireless war;
> Come and have now:
>> hunger
>> danger
>> and hate.

It was his last warning. She took it.

Whether Beatrice knew it or not, O'Neill at the time of their romance was the father of a son he had seen only once following his birth in 1910. His romance with the child's mother, Kathleen Jenkins, had gone a step farther than ardent rhetoric. She became pregnant and O'Neill married her. Neither family approved of the match, and O'Neill was sent away to rustication in Honduras. He was there when the child was born and upon his return, the two obtained a divorce. In later years, when he came to know and admire his son, he wrote to Kathleen formally, courteously, signing himself "Eugene O'Neill" as if they were only acquaintances.

In the years to follow were two romances that had important consequences. The first was with Louise Bryant, the self-emancipated "new woman" who carried on tumultuous romances with both O'Neill and John Reed, the Communist writer. There is no extant correspondence between O'Neill and Bryant. The letters were burned after Reed's death and Bryant's marriage to William C. Bullitt. Bullitt described their contents as containing "wails of despairing, unrequited love."

O'Neill was deeply, passionately committed to her. They met in 1916, about the time of his last letter to Beatrice Ashe, when she with Reed formed part of the amateur acting group that created the Provincetown Players. Bryant and Reed wrote plays for the summer theatre and she acted in O'Neill's play *Thirst* when it was staged in August. She had beauty and charm, but minimal personal honesty. She first met Reed in Portland, Oregon. Leaving her husband, she followed Reed to the east coast and lived openly with him. By the fall of 1916, the two were married, but shortly after the wedding, Reed went to Johns Hopkins Hospital for major surgery. Louise then set her cap seriously for O'Neill. She probably felt what she was doing was justified by her "modernity," her "freedom," and her sexual courage, for she instituted a ménage-à-trois with the two men. Modern and free though she was, her dishonesty came to trouble O'Neill. She did not tell Reed of her affair with O'Neill, and she tried to convince O'Neill that Reed, following his operation, was unable to have sex with her.

O'Neill's involvement was deep, but in 1917 when she went with Reed to the U.S.S.R. O'Neill gave her up. In 1918, when she returned, leaving Reed abroad, she again sought out O'Neill. But his life had changed. He was by then married, and his rejection of her, although not easy, was final.

In 1917, O'Neill, suffering one suspects, from a severe case of "rebound" after Bryant's departure met a young writer, Agnes Boulton, at the Hell Hole, a saloon in Greenwich Village. Many said that she looked like Louise Bryant, although she was gentler with the kind of demure look that reminded some observers of Rossetti's Blessed Damozel with whom O'Neill had earlier compared Beatrice Ashe. Without long preliminaries, such was the bohemian freedom from sexual restriction that O'Neill found in the Village, they were living together in New York and Provincetown. In April, 1918, they were married, and in October, 1919, their son Shane was born.

This was the time when O'Neill's career began in earnest. The one-act plays produced by the Provincetown Players when they moved to New York had been the start, but in the fall of 1919, he was negotiating with professional, on-Broadway managers for the production of his first mature, full-length plays, *Beyond the Horizon,* and *Chris Christophersen,* the play that later became *"Anna Christie."* The correspondence with Agnes, therefore, is intermittent, written as O'Neill moved from Peaked Hill Bar on Cape Cod to New York to West Point Pleasant, New Jersey, where Agnes's family had a home. En route to New York from Provincetown on the night boat, unable to get a cabin, he sat up writing her:

I've got to the end of all the reading matter I want to read. Will have to take out the rest of the night with dreams of you (waking!). I'll go out now and do this properly by watching the sea—our sea—the same that laps the front yard of our Peaked Hill Bar. I love you, My Own! I miss you! I wish the devil I were back in Happy Home this minute—(not only for the sake of a place to flop)

One listens in vain for the passionate rhetoric of the letters to Beatrice. Domesticity creeps in like frost. She is away from Provincetown, and he writes:

I am writing this on the [typewriter] because I seem to have caught more cold last night and have acquired the damndest stiff neck ever. At that it is just as well it is my neck because I can do something for that, even though you are absent, while if it were—but I will whisper the rest when I see you. Loneliness makes me Rabelaisian.

I have made a revolutionary decision. Walking this p.m. my legs were frozen. So will you get me at Lord and Taylors six pairs of long drawers, three medium and three heavy....

Worked hard today on fourth scene—hope to finish it tomorrow. All love to you, Own Dear Little Wife! I am lonely. I need you.

The letters and telegrams that fill the correspondence in the ensuing years are concerned for the most part with an extraordinary phase of his career. Between 1920 and 1926, sixteen of his plays were produced in New York City. Overseeing their staging, he was kept in a turmoil. Five times, two of his plays opened within a month of one another. He joined with his friends Robert Edmond Jones and Kenneth Macgowan as manager of the Provincetown Playhouse. And the writing never stopped. Plays poured from him and the energy of creation replaced the delights of epistolary romance,

In 1924, he and Agnes moved to Bermuda and the distance set the correspondence in motion once again. One night, while she was away visiting her family, he wrote her a letter more intense than usual:

Own, Own Wife:

God, how I miss you! and how horribly alone I have felt ever since returning here! I actually broke down on the bed in our room in a fit of hysterical crying when I first went up there. I know this is unreasonable, a bit absurd when you are only going to be gone a week, but my whole control seems gone and my inner being is in pretty shattered shape. *I need you, need you, need you!*—intensely more now than ever before in our married life. I feel—it's so hard to attempt to explain—as if this were a crucial period in my life, an ordeal, a test on which everything I have built depended—God knows what!—and our lives were in the balance. And it's so bitterly hard to be alone—although I know your love is here with me and in that faith I can come through.

This sounds incoherent. Well, I feel that way. But don't be frightened.

There's no danger of anything you might fear. I'm just alone and miserable, and will be until your return.

Because I love you! Remember and think over our talk last night.

I kiss your dear lips and body. Your lover always.

What Agnes had to fear was not insubstantial despite his self-reassuring protestations of eternal passion, for in October of the previous year, 1926, another correspondence was initiated. In New York City, he wrote:

Dear Carlotta:

And your fine note did me more good than you can imagine! To know that our luncheon meant something to you means a lot to me. The shoe is on my foot. I am the one to be grateful!

Don't *you* talk about "extra veronal!" You *are!* You don't—or at any rate you shouldn't!—need those futile embellishments we others have to adorn our egos with in order to strut successfully before our mirrors. *You're* splendid!

I'm sorry I can't make the luncheon. I will miss not seeing you. But let's get together again soon. I'll call you up tomorrow—I mean Monday—morning and try to catch you. I tried it this a.m. and yesterday. What do you do going out so early? I suspect you must be in love with a milkman! Or am I a late riser?

O'Neill, involved increasingly with productions, was now travelling frequently between Bermuda and New York City. In New York, he saw Carlotta Monterey often, their affair achieved an intimacy and ardor, and what Agnes had to fear became substantial. In November, 1926, he wrote as he sailed for Bermuda:

Dearest:

She's starting to roll now, off the Hook. I remember in my sailor days what a thrill of living it gave me, that first feel of the great ground swell of ocean heaving under me.... Now that old thrill is gone. The ground swell is just a swell. The rhythm is lost. The self that it excited to dreams was long since buried at sea. But there are times when, lolling on deck as a passenger I can feel it swimming under the keel of the ship, the haunting soul of a drowned one, wailing lamentable sagas of the past and mocking me in the blasphemous irony of the forecastle: "What did they give yer, Gene the Yank, in place of the sea?" "Oh," I answer with forced airiness, "There's a little fame, you know; and I once heard that someone once told someone that fame is sweet to the taste." "It don't go down with me, that tale," he retorts, "and it don't go down with the sea neither, 'ceptin' down in it to drown and dissolve." "Well," I say defensively, I've got a little money and a little house and a little security and ease." "And cauliflowers in the front yard? But there's roses deep in the sea," he answers. "Aw, hell. What has it got yuh? This thing's still in your inside but it ain't your belly. It's way down—" etc. And so on. Quite like the Hairy Ape, that long-drowned self of mine, who comes back to haunt my loneliest bitterest hours. Today I said to him: "There's Carlotta." And I hear him give what sounded like a grunt of approval and say something like "Even a god-damned fool sometimes finds his rightful harbor at last." And he went away.

The letter continues to speak of his despair at leaving Carlotta and of his feeling that God has slammed the door and left his prison in darkness. The ship is taking him back to Bermuda, toward Agnes. To write so dejectedly is "rank ingratitude for the great rare joy your love has given me...only just now you seem so far away, so lost to me. If I could only kiss you again, Carlotta—" And then a postscript: she has sent him a cable, and "it was as if your presence became suddenly apparent in my cabin, and I could hear your voice saying that everything will come out as we wish it." And he claims, "I am full of faith again.... I hope the roses pleased you. I wanted each one to be a prophecy to you of an hour to come to us." He concludes:

I think I shall have to tell the truth right from the start down here. It will be kinder to all in the end. I am a bad liar, even by omission, and I can't live a lie. My silences have a way of being more damning than words. And there is no such thing as the saving lie. Only the truth can save us.... Oh, I don't know what I'll do. I am so tortured now I can't trust my own judgment.... What did—or do—you think I ought to do? Please tell me! You have a much better head for this than I. You are strong and cool when you want to be. I should have asked you. It seems now I was so unpardonably vague. It was all so beautifully cataclysmic for me. Everything in the world but you seemed as remote as if it were in another life, a past life. But now, mile by mile it grows exigently into a present that I must live and grin and work in—attempt to,— at least—for what?—we will all be dead soon and good deeds and bad will become but a faint echo of one same deed, heard for a moment or two.

To Agnes, at Christmas time, 1927, he wrote:

I will not beat about the bush but come to the point at once. I love someone else. Most deeply. There is no possible doubt of this.... We have often promised each other that if one ever came to the other and said they loved someone else that we would understand, that we would know that love is something which cannot be denied or argued with, that it must be faced. And that is what I am asking you to understand and know now. I am sure that I could accept the inevitable in that spirit if our roles were reversed. And I know that you, if for nothing else than that you just remember with kindness our years of struggle together and that I have tried to make you happy and be happy with you, will act with the same friendship toward me. After all, you know that I have always been faithful to you, that I have never gone seeking love, that if my love for you had not died no new love would have come to me.... If you are frank and look into your own heart you will find no real love left for me in it. What has bound us together for the past few years has been deep down a fine affection and friendship, and this I shall always feel for you.

There have been moments when our old love flared into life again but you must acknowledge that these have grown steadily rarer. On the other side of the ledger moments of a very horrible hate have been more and more apparent, a poisonous bitterness and resentment, a cruel desire to wound, rage and frustration and revenge. This has killed our chance for happiness together. There have been too many insults to pride and self-respect, too many torturing scenes that one may forgive but which something in one cannot forget and which no love, however strong, can continue to endure and live.

O'Neill and Carlotta wrote mutually exploring one another. He told her:

I...long to hear you "go on and on" about what you are to do in your strange life. Has it been so strange? From the expression I've seen sometimes in your eyes I should imagine so—but I really know so precious little—but the little *is* precious—about you, do you know it?

And there was some self-deception:

What did I mean when I wrote that I had been perfectly frank? Just that! As soon as I reached here I told Agnes exactly how I felt about leaving you. I said I loved you. I also said, and with equal truth, that I loved her. Does this sound idiotic to you? I hope not! I hope you will understand. If you should not, it means we had better—stop, while forgetting is not so horribly impossible as it might be (for me) later. It is possible to love like that. Perhaps you know this as well as I. You are not one of the simple, one-track ones who are so lucky as always to be able to know but one thing at a time. And there are people and things one cannot tear out of one's life without leaving a wound that sickens not only one's own future but the future of everyone whose life is close to one afterward....

But I suppose you are curious about Agnes. She has been very fine about it. She has offered to do anything about it I want—to set me free, etc.

etc. However, it is ridiculous to imagine one can ever set another person free—and it is equally asinine to imagine one can set oneself free by one's own efforts. Either the thing resolves itself inside one in silence, and the freeing moment comes—or it doesn't. And who can foretell?

And what would I do with freedom? And what would you do with my freedom, Strange Carlotta—granting, which I have no particular reason to expect, that you would want to be bothered with it at all? It is true I love you but I do not know you. You are so strange and beautiful to me. And I am horribly confused about all this.... It takes time—time—time—to remember—or to forget—to take this road—or that.

One supposes that Carlotta turned the screws, subtly but not too gently. O'Neill writes her, "It seems at times as if all the suffering I find in your letters were my fault." Or again, "You speak about fighting alone against all the things that you want to do." She starts to learn to type: "Why are you taking up the Corona? Are you thinking of doing some writing again?" And then he takes the bait: "Or if you'll add shorthand to the Corona, I'll offer you a marvellous position as a private secretary." She made contact with Eugene Junior and sent a birthday present to Shane. She sent O'Neill a photograph of her portrait and copies of poems by Keats and Verlaine. Ultimately, in the summer of 1927, she tried absence and withdrew, going for a "cure" at Baden-Baden.

O'Neill, hard at work on the final draft of *Strange Interlude*, found time to write her, but the letters lacked the passion of the earlier correspondence:

I want so much to see you again! Your last letter—but one—sounded so unhappy and lonely. I wish we could talk together. There is something rotten and wrong about all this. I feel as if you were going out of my life forever and that there was nothing I could do, in fairness, to hold you. We write and write and we never mention love except as a conventional tail to letters, and act like two shy defensive people who are in deadly fear of being wounded. Do

I dare believe you still love me—that you ever did love me? I look at your letters and wonder and doubt and am afraid and slink back into myself....I want you in my life but I know I am losing you.

In the Fall, when he went to New York City to confer about the staging of the play, love returned like the tide. She was now called "Shadow Eyes," the name taken from Arthur Symon's translation of Baudelaire, and on the ship back to Bermuda, he wrote "This is hell—but I remember Heaven as past and a future." Passion returned to the letters:

Dear, there is nothing to write except the same thing over and over: I love you! There is only a great empty ache for you left of me! Remember that ache! It is yours.

I am getting all brown again. I lie in the sun and dream of you in the warm air—your warmth...air of my life warmed to new life by your sweetness and beauty!

In November, 1927, coming back to New York for rehearsals of the play, he made a date with her for the evening his boat docked, and told her "I will be alone." He suggested that they find some form of physical exercise to do together ("Oh yes, I know! But I meant outdoor exercise!"), and he concluded, "I have been feeling pretty blue and disintegrated and harried and restless. There is no peace except in your arms."

He never returned to Bermuda. January, 1928 saw the productions of both *Marco Millions* and *Strange Interlude,* and in February, he and Carlotta left for Europe where they were to remain for the next three years.

To Agnes now, he wrote concerning their divorce and, since *Strange Interlude* had proved to be one of the notorious successes of the New York theatre, made suggestions as to how to avoid damaging press coverage. As Agnes enlisted legal talent, and as he came to feel that she on the strength of the play's success was trying to take him for all he was worth, O'Neill proved vituperative beyond rational measure. He set detectives on her and had her past investigated. He questioned the legitimacy of her first marriage and of her daughter by that marriage. He wondered whether his own marriage was legal, his own children bastards. Until late in life, when his anger at her had turned to ashes, he referred to her as "that woman," and "that Bitch," and he blamed her unceasingly for the derelictions (as he felt them to be) of Shane and Oona.

Carlotta was a different woman from the bohemian Agnes. She had come from Oakland, California, the daughter of a Danish farmer. She had been educated not only in California, but also in Europe, in Paris and London, where she attended Sir Herbert Beerbohm Tree's Academy of Dramatic Arts. Her beauty had helped her carve out a minor stage career, but her major occupation proved to be fostering the genius of her husband. She had been thrice married, the third time to the artist Ralph Barton, whose cartoons were significant features of the magazines of the 1920's. For Barton, whom she had met in 1922, she proved to be a caring, loving companion who devoted herself to creating a world in which he could work to the fullest extent of his energy and talent. From him, she may have learned some matters of style, particularly in the decoration of elegant rooms, a talent which she would ultimately display to the full in the homes she provided for O'Neill. She divorced Barton early in 1926, charging him with infidelity.

Barton's love for her continued, and when she and O'Neill were married and returned from Europe to New York City, Barton shot himself. His suicide note spoke sadly of his "beautiful, lost angel, Carlotta, the only woman I have ever loved."

What she had been for Barton she became for O'Neill, a caretaker who protected and fostered him and his work, giving him her life in an extraordinary act of devotion.

It was a marriage founded on love and faith, but at times it was shaken by differences of temperament and by outer circumstances. The first real crisis occurred in 1929. After they had spent some time in London and in southern France, they took a cruise to the Orient. There, O'Neill fell off the wagon after a period of abstinence. In Shanghai, they fought, and he struck her. She left the hotel and took a different ship, the S. S. *Monroe,* to return to Europe. Astutely, she left behind on their first ship, the S. S. *Coblenz,* her Swedish maid, Tuwe Drew, who wired her daily reports of his condition:

STILL DRINKING / FURIOUS WITH ME / DONT WORRY / DOCTOR VISITED / DIDNT SAY YOUR WHEREABOUTS / PROMISED DRINK NO MORE IF YOU JOIN HIM IN EUROPE FOLLOWING MESSAGE GIVEN DOCTOR / DEAREST FORGIVE ME BUT NEED YOUR HELP MORE THAN EVER BEFORE BECAUSE I AM HALF MAD WITH UTTER LONELINESS WITHOUT FRIENDS OR PLANS OR HOPE / TUWE HAS NEVER BEEN NEAR ME / IT WOULD BE TREMENDOUS HELP IF YOU CABLE ME EVERY DAY / I LOVE YOU AND I DESERVE THAT / THE DOCTOR HAS MY PROMISE AND I WILL KEEP IT / HOW ARE YOU / I FEEL SO TERRIBLY WORRIED ABOUT YOU

Suddenly a miracle!

POSSIBILITY COBLENZ MAY BE DELAYED PORT SUDAN / SHIP WILL BE IN PORT SAID SAME TIME AS MONROE / IF SO LET US ARRANGE TALK SOMEHOW / IF ONLY FIVE MINUTES THIS WOULD MEAN EVERYTHING IN THE WORLD TO ME DEAREST ONE

But then it is touch and go whether the ships will be in port simultaneously, and O'Neill gets an idea:

IT PROMISES TO BE NARROW MARGIN BUT I WILL MAKE IT OR WHAT DO YOU THINK OF MY CHANGING TO MONROE IF AC-

COMMODATIONS / TAKING ALL HAND LUGGAGE LEAVING
TRUNKS TO TUWE TO BOND THROUGH.

And she said yes, and they lived happily ever after, for a time.

Shortly thereafter, they settled in France, he hard at work on *Dynamo* and *Mourning Becomes Electra*. When Agnes's divorce was final, they married in Paris and a quiet domesticity set in. Occasionally, one or the other made a trip alone to Paris. Love letters marked such occasions. He called her, surprisingly,

Darling Fatbum:

...I am most lonely and sitting here dreaming of you —and it is pouring outside as it has been ever since lunch time.... What else shall I tell you? That I love you with everything in me? You know that. That I miss you terribly? You ought to know that too but I don't think you realize how much. It is as if I were one-half of a Siamese twins that had just been amputated apart! A lost feeling! The house is so big and still. I keep looking up expecting to see you sitting in the chair near me. I feel a hungry longing to reach out and touch your knee or your foot—or say "time for a caress!" and get up and put my arms around you and nuzzle in and kiss your neck—or sit on the cushion at your feet and feel your arms pressing me so tenderly against your breast—or simply look up when you're not looking, as I so often do, and think how beautiful and sweet you are and how lucky I am!

He worried at times about his silences when she was with him and about the work he was doing:

Your letters make me feel so unworthy, make me conscious of how often I fail you—or seem to fail you—when I drift around moody with preoccupations about work or worrying about this or that unimportant irritation. But you must forgive this as only an eccentricity of me. For deep in my being, possessing my whole being, is always you! I never dreamed I could love anyone as much as I love you! The idea of life without you beside me, in me, through me, part of me, would be impossible now. You are my life! And you must feel that even my work is a part of you too since it is the expression of the I who am you!…

I feel "Dynamo," in a sense, wronged us—not because critics panned it, that means nothing, they have panned some of my best stuff, but because I felt myself it was a step back, not a step forward, and so did not represent what you are to me.

Mourning Becomes Electra was a different matter, and he dedicated the play to her as his "mother and wife and mistress and friend!—and collaborator!"

She remained these to him when they returned to New York, in Georgia, and at Tao House in California. When he was in a hospital in Oakland and she went east to sell their Georgia home, he arranged for her to receive a dozen red roses on her return trip, at Chicago, Omaha, Utah, and a gala two dozen at the Fairmont Hotel when she reached San Francisco. Telegrams accompanied the flowers to cheer her homecoming.

At Tao House, living in close companionship, the correspondence thinned down to Christmas cards, and anniversary and birthday poems sometimes adorned with phallic sketches of a small black cat: "Darling One: Every day, in every way, you are more and more beautiful & I love you more! Your Gene." And the card is decorated with the black cats at the four corners. At Christmas, 1945, when the tremor made writing almost impossible, in a shattered handwriting he told her "After the 'afternoons gray and smoky' may our evenings be 'yellow and rose.' Let us pray! All my love, Sweetheart."

On their anniversary, July 22, 1946, he managed to write:

Sweetheart,
With the same old love deep in my heart I felt for you on that day in Paris, 1929!

I wish you could say the same, forgiving as I forgive all the mistakes and injuries done one to another through thoughtlessness or lack of understanding.

In justice, as everyone but ourselves seems to know, our marriage has been the most successful and happy of any we know—until late years.

Here's for a new beginning! All my love and [here the handwriting disintegrates.]

The silencing of his creative work by the tremor occasioned the trouble. The war made Tao House uninhabitable, and he was aware of her problems: she was ill, weakened by an eye operation, in pain with a back disorder, and the marriage was often in trouble. Once his eye strayed to a pretty young typist, and, as to Beatrice Ashe long before, he wrote a poem about their walk on a beach. It was a harmless, platonic affair, but it occasioned some difficulty. When the O'Neills returned to the east, there were several serious quarrels, occasioned for the most part by their increasing illnesses. Several times separations were urged on O'Neill by his friends, but inevitably, once he was able, he returned to Carlotta:

For the love of God, forgive and come back. You are all I have in life. I am sick and I will surely die without you.

On their anniversary in 1948, He wrote:

Darling:...You have been life to me, and the greatest beauty and joy, and without you I am nothing. Please, Sweetheart, I have been through hell and you have. I could never again act as I have acted. I love you Darling. Darling, I love you! I love you! I am yours! Don't leave me!

There was one more serious rift, but again he fought his way back to her despite the many hands that tried to separate them. In July,

1953, a few months before he died, he wrote her for the last time, a dedication to *A Moon for the Misbegotten,* and they are the words of a man who truly had found faith and love in marriage:

> To darling Carlotta my wife, who for twenty-three years has endured my rotten nerves, my lack of stability, my general cussedness, with love and understanding—This token of my gratitude and awareness—a poor thing— a play she dislikes, and which I have come to loathe—dating back to 1944— my last. I am old and would be sick of life, were it not that you are here as deep and understanding in your love as ever—and I as deep in my love for you as when we stood in the Première Arrondissment on July 22, 1929 and both said faintly "Oui."

Love's Labors Dispossessed:
The Complexities of a Friendship

N ot every marriage is made in heaven. People may be joined together in many unlikely places, even in a publishing house, where on rare occasions an author and an editor can meet in mutual trust, bred of professional competence, friendship, interdependence, and a shared participation in a creative process. Or, as Eugene O'Neill put it, inscribing a copy of *The Iceman Cometh* to his editor Saxe Commins, in "love and admiration and respect."

The association that was to become a lifelong intimacy probably began in New York City in late 1915 and was affirmed during the summer of 1916 at Provincetown on Cape Cod, when both men were drawn into the enthusiastic playmaking of the dedicated amateurs who were shortly to form the Provincetown Players. Commins went to the Cape to join his sister Stella and her husband, a young actor named E.J. Ballantine. Stella appeared in the Players' production of George Cram Cook's *Change Your Style*, and Ballantine acted in, and later claimed to have directed, their memorable first performance of O'Neill's *Bound East for Cardiff*. The Ballantines were signers of the first "constitution" of the Players, and, although Stella's participation as an actress was short-lived, her husband appeared in a number of the New York productions of the group. Commins's contribution that summer was prophetic. He typed Susan Glaspell's play *Trifles*, an early editorial service of the kind he was later to perform for O'Neill.

Saxe Commins was O'Neill's editor at Random House and a life-long friend. This essay was written in 1985 as a forward to Love and Admiration and Respect, *the O'Neill-Commins Correspondence. Ed. Dorothy Commins. (Duke University Press, Durham, N. C., 1986) Reprinted by permission.*

At the University of Pennsylvania, during the time of World War I, Commins inhaled the odor of ferment that was to result in the heady intellectual wine of the 1920s. Like many young men whose interests ranged beyond the ordinary goals of middle-class America, he gravitated when occasion permitted to Greenwich Village, where, it appeared, all that was new was being tested for validity in argument and art. He has not recorded the course of his *vie de bohème* in detail, but he maintained his contact with the Players. His unlauded lost play, *The Obituary*, closed a three-play bill at the Provincetown Playhouse in December 1916. O'Neill's *Before Breakfast* had been staged by the group earlier in the same month.

What drew the two men together, if indeed there was at first any special bond, can only be surmised. Commins's friendly intelligence and an eagerness to learn about many things made him attractive. As Emma Goldman's nephew, he no doubt gained entrée into the circle of radical experimenters of whom O'Neill for a time made one. In his turn, he perhaps responded to a wildness in O'Neill, an untamed masculinity that was a far cry from what he had known in the warmly communal Jewish family in Rochester, N.Y., where he had his roots. O'Neill had a remarkable aptitude for making friends among men of all social levels and interests; Commins had an aptitude for listening and for making intelligent and amusing commentaries on the world around him. He had a love of literature that even in its youthful stages would have appealed to the more or less self-educated O'Neill.

The first substantial account of their association is contained in a series of letters O'Neill wrote to his wife, Agnes, when he left her in Provincetown to visit Commins in Rochester. By 1921 Commins, who had studied dentistry, had established a successful practice in his hometown. O'Neill's teeth were a disaster area. He arrived for treatments on April 21 and was taken to meet the elder Comminses, with whom Saxe lived. He found them to be "fine, lovable people." Less lovable was the process that began that afternoon. A wisdom tooth was extracted, and, although it proved to be stubborn, O'Neill at first wrote that he felt relatively pain free. "Bridge-work," Commins said, was in order, but not "plates." On Friday, O'Neill was less cheerful. He wrote Agnes that the roots of the wisdom tooth "had grown together in a bunch making the tooth larger at the bottom than anywhere else—hence Saxe had almost to call in the derrick squad before he could budge it."

He found that he liked Saxe's family. They are "fine folks," he said again, and he appreciated their courteous hospitality. On the day of his arrival they had received a wire from Los Angeles, saying that their granddaughter had died following a tonsillectomy. Despite their sorrow, the elder Comminses welcomed O'Neill into their home.

On Saturday the drilling for the bridge-work began, continuing on Sunday, "in spite of its being the Sabbath." On Monday Saxe extracted "some old abscessed roots...a frightful ordeal.... They had grown in under the next tooth and simply refused to be yanked out—had to be cut out bit by bit—and the anesthetic didn't work right and—well it was hell on wheels, believe me. Poor Saxe! He honestly suffered more than I did about it. I'm a fine sight—jaw all swollen—and glad you can't see me. No woman could love this face."

Commins's bereaved brother and sister-in-law arrived in Rochester, and the men moved from the family home to that of Commins's sister Miriam on the outskirts of town. O'Neill rested contentedly there in a "half farm, half suburban villa...nice and quiet...woods nearby...fertile...big orchards, etc." On Thursday, April 28, another extraction was in order, but by Saturday the bridges were fabricated and, O'Neill wrote, "five or six small fillings are still in store—and then, release! The work Saxe has done has been fine and should prove lasting. It has not been painless—but I expected the worst anyway."

By the beginning of May, O'Neill had had enough, not only of the dental process but of the Commins world. He complained to Agnes of there being too much "family—crowds and crowds of them, seven or eight children running and shouting about—talk, talk, talk! a general pandemonium...all yesterday afternoon and evening. Twelve or more sitting at dinner! I nearly went 'nuts,' and writing was out of the question. But I was sort of guest of honor and had to stick it out." He stuck it out until May 4 when his treatment ended, and he returned to Agnes and the sea and the quiet of Provincetown.

For O'Neill, who had never had a family nor, it would appear, significant dental work, the double ordeal of familial affection and dental extraction proved too much. Yet something beyond the Greenwich Village friendship was born in that week. The relationship between the men moved from a level of easy familiarity to a plane of personal sympathy and gratified response: "Poor Saxe! He honestly suffered more than I did...." Throughout his life O'Neill responded to such attention as Commins paid him. All of his important friendships—as with Kenneth Macgowan and George Jean Nathan—as well as his marriage to Carlotta Monterey were based partly on a dependency, an unspoken request to be looked after and cared for. There was nothing overtly effeminate or passive in such a need. O'Neill was a man men genuinely liked. Even today he is remembered by casual laborers who worked for him on his California ranch, by Herbert Freeman, his chauffeur for many years, and by those who knew him in more fully professional ways as someone who met them as equals and treated them fairly and with reliable friendship.

However outgoing he sometimes appeared, those who knew him most closely speak of his shyness, a quality that was an outer manifestation of the deep center of his personality, that part of his being where he most fully lived and from whose fires the plays came. When he wrote, he was a different person from the friendly man for whom so many felt affection. Then he appeared abstracted, even unfriendly.

The encircling walls of his study and his own extraordinary powers of concentration walled him in physically and psychologically against intrusion. With the exception of Carlotta, no one breached those walls to enter the world of solitude and silence where the plays were created. Some, however, came near that world, and once the essential creative act was complete, were allowed participation in the final readying of the work for stage or publication. Saxe Commins was one of these few, and it is probable that no other person except Carlotta was trusted so completely or came so close to knowing the essential O'Neill. It was perhaps inevitable that he and Carlotta, whose lives were given a special meaning by their privileged service, would become rivals in their desire to protect and foster the creative core of O'Neill's being.

At first, it was friendly assistance Commins offered—talking out ideas, suggesting source books, typing, and nonprofessional editorial chores on those occasions when they were together. Later, Commins began to stand in for O'Neill at ceremonial occasions, accompanying Agnes to first nights and once, as his memoir records, serving as priest for an astonishing confession. By 1928, however, Carlotta Monterey had entered O'Neill's life and his marriage to Agnes ended. Then the relationship between the men took on a new and ultimately more professional turn. In December 1927 Commins married Dorothy Berliner, a talented pianist of great personal charm. Soon thereafter he rebelled against the life of a Rochester dentist. A man needs no reason to pack up and get out from a situation in which the profits yield nothing of the spirit. Commins wanted to write. He had recently published a collaboration with Lloyd Coleman, *Psychology, A Simplification,* but thereafter his writing was largely confined to editorial suggestions and to a variety of notes and introductions. Although in such a boom time as 1928 the freedom to look for more than Rochester offered was readily possible, for Commins it was almost too late. He was thirty-four, married, and financially "settled." Yet his wife's career needed nurturing: a year studying in Paris was an almost essential preliminary to an important career as a pianist. For a would-be writer, in those years, the lure of Paris was strong. Also, a fact to be noted as the Comminses determined to set sail for France is that they were following in O'Neill's wake. O'Neill had left New York City with Carlotta in February 1928, determined to live abroad until the divorce from Agnes was final. Certainly Commins did not sell his dental practice and go to France because of O'Neill, but his friend's romance, his somewhat adventurous journey, and the example of O'Neill's cutting off old ties may have been an encouragement. Commins's break may have seemed easier because of his friend's presence in Europe.

Whatever part O'Neill's elopement played in Commins's decision, it was not long before they met. In July, Commins went to visit O'Neill at Guéthary near Biarritz. He was invited cordially but was asked not to bring Dorothy. The letters indicate that the reason given was the presumptive embarrassment of the two women over the fact that Eugene and Carlotta were, as the phrase was, "living in sin." Commins arrived on June 21 and stayed through June 30, returning to Paris with the manuscript of the recently completed *Dynamo,* which he typed to O'Neill's full satisfaction. Shortly, as the letters reveal, he was performing a number of personal services for both O'Neills.

On August 20 Carlotta invited the Comminses to dinner at their Paris hotel, and from that time forward the relationship was fixed in orbit. Carlotta asked them to run more errands, thanked them effusively, and in tones of extravagant affection wooed them. O'Neill, beginning the long period of work on *Mourning Becomes Electra,* was more laconic, but his letters testify to the affirming friendship, based on affection, gratitude for services rendered, and growing trust. Later, in February 1929, when the O'Neills had returned from their cruise to the Orient, both the Comminses were received as guests, and to judge by the letters that remain, the social waters were unruffled.

Below the surface, however, Carlotta's private response to the visits at Guéthary and at the château at Le Plessis was less cordial. In her diary she refers to the Comminses only briefly, as "C" and "D," and most frequently she calls him "our 'guest,'" putting the term in ironic quotation marks. She notes on July 20, 1928, that "Gene & 'guest' talk out in garden until midnight—I retire at 11."

Although the Comminses surely did not arrive uninvited, she remarks on February 19, 1929, that "C & D turn up as house guests," and when the Comminses came to dinner in Paris as a result of a gracious invitation, she notes in her diary for August 25, "Our 'guests' from Guéthary turn up! They remain to dinner." What was perhaps her most affectionate letter to Commins, dated August 30, 1929, was in answer apparently to a letter from Commins that, in her diary entry of August 31, she called "idiotic."

What motivated Carlotta will never be fully comprehensible, although Commins's "idiotic" letter may provide a clue. The letter is lost, but if its contents can be inferred from her reply, it concerned some of O'Neill's friends from the Village days, particularly the Provincetown stage director James Light, his wife, and Eleanor Fitzgerald, the former guardian and overseer of the Players. Carlotta viewed this group of old friends with suspicion and antipathy. They remembered and called to an O'Neill she had not known and brought back a time from which she had attempted to divorce the playwright. Saxe Commins, in a way, belonged to that group. What he represented to her, therefore, was at first an intruder from a past she did not wish to acknowledge. Furthermore, as his services to O'Neill increased, and as O'Neill talked with him late into the night, he appeared to be moving closer to the center of O'Neill's creative life. The ironic quotation marks of the diary entries may reveal a jealousy, a dawning feeling that he was becoming her rival.

Carlotta Monterey was a temperamental, spoiled, sophisticated, imperious, handsome woman. Her tastes, formed in New York City and London, were a defense against her origins in Oakland, California. Like many men and women, she used her marriages and her love affairs to propel herself up and out of a world she found stultifying. Her rise, although it was achieved by a different form of transport, had a similar motivation to that of Commins when he left Rochester. Her career as an actress was ephemeral and secondary to her appearances in a somewhat hazily defined social milieu. She acted in nothing but rubbish until 1922, when she was cast in the on-Broadway production of *The Hairy Ape,* replacing the actress who had created the role in the Village theatre. That the respected, uptown producer Arthur Hopkins used her in the short but crucial role suggests that she had some ability and that her name had drawing power. The theatre, however, offered her little more than a temporary standing place. It was not her future.

When she and O'Neill met again, in Maine during the summer of 1926, the acquaintance, which had earlier been fractious since she was an unwelcome alien among the Provincetown group, became warmer. Their liaison at the Belgrade lakes continued throughout the next year, and O'Neill saw in her something more than a passing summer love. He was at work on two plays that signaled a change in quality and direction from his earlier work, *Lazarus Laughed* and *Strange Interlude.* Neither could be produced with the facilities offered by the Village theatres, which to this time had been adequate to his needs. As the horizons of his playwriting expanded, he began to think of major stars as his actors—Katharine Cornell and Feodor Chaliapin, to name two. He made an alliance with the Theatre Guild, which was shortly to stage both *Marco Millions* and *Strange Interlude.* Seeking more profound forms of dramatic statement, he was entering a new world and, as he approached forty, a new life.

He came to think of Carlotta as essential to that life. What O'Neill asked of her was that she give up everything she had gained—her career, her friends, the comforts of her known world—and become his protectress, or, as he said in the dedication to *Mourning Becomes Electra,* his "mother, and wife and mistress and friend!—And collaborator!" She was to become the guardian of his creative life, as Agnes, with a more casual style of living in a more carefree time, had never become. Carlotta knew well what he asked of her, and she accepted the bargain, keeping faithfully to it for so long as the marriage remained vital.

The center of the marriage was his writing. His plays became her *raison d'être*. They were her pride and in a measure her love. As she loved the man, she loved and served his work, making no separation between the two. To Agnes, O'Neill once wrote in some bitterness, "Excuse me for speaking so much about my plays. I realize it's tactless on my part. It's quite evident to me that you're not interested since you never mention them." He would never have written such an accusation to Carlotta. She stood close to him as he wrote, moving from his side only to position herself at the gates to turn away all persons she felt might intrude on the quiet world where he could write undisturbed. She built homes to give him comfort and peace, and she willingly endured the lonely, mute days while he worked. She nursed him in his increasingly severe illnesses. She provided diversion when he needed it and warded it off when in her judgment it was unwelcome. The criterion *was* her judgement. There was no one else, for O'Neill made few decisions about the outward conduct of their lives together. Thus, in her judgment, the past was distraction. O'Neill's animosity toward Agnes for not making possible a rapid divorce was intense. Carlotta set her sword against all that Agnes represented, with the result that many of O'Neill's old friends—the drinking cronies, the Village theatre people—were turned away. Agnes's children were continual problems, and, although Carlotta received them, she did so with an inner reluctance, akin to the irony with which she at first received the Comminses. O'Neill let it happen; his love for Carlotta was great and his trust in her complete.

No doubt, she felt a certain vanity at being "Mrs. Eugene O'Neill, the wife of America's greatest playwright," but she does not appear to have capitalized on her position. Instead, she entered the silence with him. Her withdrawal to France, thence to Casa Genotta in Georgia and to Tao House in California, was as complete as his. The marriage was not easy to achieve, but together they found the way to its fulfillment in the Tao House plays, which were nurtured through great physical hardship in times of national and familial stress. She was jealous. How could she not be? Jealousy is a concomitant of dedication. Nurses are jealous; mothers are jealous; lovers, wives, agents, even editors are jealous of those they love and serve.

When, at the height of his creative powers, O'Neill was silenced by the tremor that made writing impossible, the marriage lost its central fire. Carlotta then had to care for a man who could no longer create, one who had become feeble and bitter and suddenly old. She herself was ill and stranded on a remote California hillside in a war-rationed world, forced to struggle for a living that was increasingly burdensome and meaningless.

At this point in their lives, bizarre jealousies arose, passing rumors of infidelities were heard, and the final tragic years began. Through them all, Carlotta attempted to keep out intruders, as she had always done, but her desperation was evident, and, as her own illness drove her to excess, she became manic in her attempt to keep everyone away from the ruin of their marriage and themselves. Decisively she drove away all of the lesser guardians. His producer Lawrence Langner, his friends Kenneth Macgowan and Sophus Winther, his publisher Bennett Cerf were cast out. O'Neill's children were shut away, and he who had perhaps been closest to O'Neill's central life, the faithful Saxe Commins, received blows whose motivation he did not understand, but which scarred his well-being and his trust in human relations until his death.

Commins, once he had found his true métier in the editorial position O'Neill procured for him with his publisher, Horace Liveright, became an intelligent, scrupulous professional. As the letters show, he protected O'Neill from loss when the Liveright firm went bankrupt, a service O'Neill repaid by insisting that Commins be hired at Random House as part of the agreement he signed with his new publisher, Bennett Cerf. In his new position Commins came fully into his own. Cerf described him as "one of the great men at Random House, a wonderful man." He was, in fact, one of the most distinguished editors in American literary history.

As an editor, Commins made many friends among the major authors of the time, but none was so close to him as O'Neill, after whom he named his son, and for whom he performed special chores, such as typing the manuscript of *The Iceman Cometh,* a job whose routine difficulty was compounded by O'Neill's microscopic handwriting, already palsy-twitched. His care of the manuscripts, especially that of *Long Day's Journey into Night,* was exemplary, providing full testimony to his unceasing concern for O'Neill's personal and literary welfare, even after the dramatist was dead.

Can there be two zealous guardians of the same person? Perhaps, so long as the one being guarded is able to mitigate potential friction. As O'Neill's strength ebbed, however, such control as he might have exerted became weakened, and, as the Commins letters and memoir shockingly reveal, suddenly Commins and Carlotta were face to face, and she was brutal. Commins recoiled in moral horror from an enemy he had not known he possessed.

He had not seen in the woman who wrote letters with such effusive grace the fierce strength of purpose born of the renunciation of everything for a single good, nor did he understand the psychological strain such renunciation causes when that single good is called in question. He was not, apparently, aware of the illnesses—among others, a form of bromide poisoning—that led her to uncontrollably manic behavior.* He had no sympathy for a woman who, with nothing left

---

*Potassium bromide, prescribed extensively in the nineteenth and early twentieth centuries as a nostrum for nervous conditions, and still occasionally found in nerve tonics and headache remedies, is only slowly excreted by the kidneys. If taken with frequency, it can reach a toxic level in the body over a period of weeks. Among the symptoms of "bromide intoxication" are irritability and emotional disturbances leading occasionally to a form of mania. (Cf. Louis Sanford Goodman and Alfred Gilman, *The Pharmacological Basis of Therapeutics* (New York, The Macmillan Co., 1941) pp. 129-131.

ahead in life, clung in despair to the shards of what had been her pride—the broken, passive man she once had loved.

At the end the outcry against Carlotta from those who had loved O'Neill became full-throated in its hatred, and the picture that Commins draws of her in his memoir has attained a legendary "truth." Commins, with Dorothy at his side, undertook to take O'Neill to their home to care for him. Carlotta, long before the plan was in evidence, sensed his rivalry. Her paranoia caused in her the inexplicable, melodramatic behavior Commins describes: the mysterious disappearance of the manuscripts, her insane behavior as O'Neill with a broken leg lay helpless in a snowstorm, the obscenities, the libelous attacks on Commins's honesty, the irrational rejection of every seeming invasion of their "privacy," no matter what the occasion.

Such action as the Comminses describe is inexcusable, but perhaps there is not so great a need for excuse as there is for understanding. At the last Commins calls Carlotta "evil," for "good" and "evil" were terms habitual to his way of thinking. O'Neill's judgment is significantly different. He said to Commins, "Try to understand. She's sick, terribly sick." What needs to be understood about the O'Neills at the end of their lives together is that in a demented and frenzied way, she was attempting to do what she had always done—serve her husband.

Two matters should be noted. After the terrifying night at Marblehead, when O'Neill was taken to a hospital and Carlotta was removed for psychiatric examination, O'Neill's first effort from his hospital bed was to dictate a letter to Carlotta, assuring her of his love and continuing concern for her welfare. Removed from her "influence" by his friends and transferred to a New York hospital, he returned immediately to her side once he was able to travel, despite the arguments and the pleas that he leave her. The second matter concerns his relationship with Eugene O'Neill, Jr., in whose career he had taken particular pride. The son had failed in his efforts to find a more glamorous career than teaching classics at Yale University, and had come far down in the world, jobless, drinking, relying on his father for support. Commins, who heard the account only from the younger O'Neill, implies that Carlotta prevented Eugene, Jr., from reaching his father at a time when he needed his signature as co-signer on a small mortgage note. Thus, Commins suggests, Carlotta was responsible for the fact that soon thereafter Eugene, Jr. committed suicide. There exist, however, two letters, one undated and written painfully in O'Neill's shaking hand, the other typed, presumably by Carlotta, dated February 25, 1950, and signed "Father" by O'Neill. The former was sent to the younger O'Neill's lawyer on March 7, 1949, and forwarded as its envelope attests. The second was sent on February 25, 1950 directly to the son. Both were covering letters for notes that O'Neill had endorsed. Carlotta did not interfere.

After O'Neill's death, when Carlotta assumed control of his literary estate and arranged for the publication and production of *Long Day's Journey into Night,* she was again viewed as a villainess transgressing against O'Neill's dying wishes that the play be withheld from publication for twenty-five years. Yet with considerable theatrical acumen, she saw that the play was carefully presented to the public. She arranged that it should first be produced in Stockholm, where the personal revelations would be of less interest than the play itself. Starring in it, and thus ensuring not only definitive performance but an aware and interested world press, were the actors from the Swedish National Theatre, many of whom were becoming international stars through the films of Ingmar Bergman. With this rather elaborate "out-of-town tryout," she then brought *Long Day's Journey into Night* into New York partly presold by the Swedish production as an unusual work of art and saw that it had a superb cast and sympathetic direction. The production in November 1956, together with the revival at Circle-in-the-Square of *The Iceman Cometh* earlier that year, began the O'Neill renaissance, restoring him to the position he had abdicated after the production of *Days Without End* in 1934—

that of "America's greatest playwright." No doubt, in a measure, Carlotta's former pride of place was also restored.

The production and her arrangement for the preservation of his literary remains was her last important service to her husband. In coincidental parallelism with his friend, Commins, who had been born six years later than O'Neill, died six years following his death. His love was unabated; his bitterness unassuaged.

II
About the Plays

The Empowering Sea

*Children of the Sea:
The Moon of the Caribbees
Bound East for Cardiff
In the Zone
The Long Voyage Home
The Emperor Jones
Little Orphan *"Anna Christie"*
The Hairy Ape

About *The Iceman Cometh* and *Hughie*
Dreams of Joy, Dreams of Pain
About *A Touch of the Poet*
The Monastery and The Prison

---

*Brief commentaries provided for radio versions of O'Neill's early sea plays and *The Emperor Jones,* recorded by BARD Productions for broadcast over National Public Radio. Printed by permission of B.A.R.D., Berkeley, California.

The Empowering Sea

The sea, they say, is in our life blood, its saline energies deeply reminding us of the life-giving, birth-inducing warmth in which we generated and from which we emerged after an eons-long life below consciousness. The sea forms an ancestral bondage, linking men and women in dim memories of a time when, without will, they belonged to its sway and were controlled by its power.

To understand their bondage and the force that compels them, human beings are sometimes drawn toward the sea with a deep yearning. Robert Frost described the walkers on the shore who turn their backs on the land and look at the sea all day:

> They cannot look out far
> They cannot look in deep.
> But when was that ever a bar
> To any watch they keep?

Trying to look far out and deep within reveals our need for the sea—a reaching back, a desire not to possess (for who can own the sea as he owns land?), but to be possessed, to return to an origin where all the problems of our conscious life undergo a deep sea-change and all conflicts are resolved in dreaming certitude, like death, like God. "I never saw the sea," said Emily Dickinson. Yet she knew what a wave must be, and it brought into her mind the certainty of heaven.

We cannot, quite, explain the desire to return, because the desire lies out of the path of rational understanding and can only be sensed from the edges of the mind, as land through which a fast-moving train passes is

A paper read to an audience at the Longwharf Theatre, New Haven, Connecticut at the time of their production of "Anna Christie," 1990.

sensed as a blur at the corner of the eye. All our will, our upward physical thrusting, our inventiveness has pulled us from the sea, and we have learned to climb impudent mountains because they are "there," forgetting that these same mountains were once thrust from the floors of prehistoric seas. We, who are the sea's creatures, live in ambiguous relationship with our parent, yearning toward and pulling away from the god-inhabited, wine-dark sea, the cruel sea, the sea around us.

Looking back in our history, we can readily call the role of men who have had a special relationship to the sea, who have responded to what they felt to be the "challenge" of the sea and sailed on it as if on horseback, into the unknown, with only an inch or so of planking to saddle them from the possessing waters: Ulysses, Leif Erikson, Columbus, Drake, Magellan, Cook—the unforgettable roster of explorers can still stir our blood. To them, as to Chichester and Heyerdahl and others nearer our time, the sea was a pathway, a means to some end—to home, as with Ulysses, to riches as with the seekers after Cathay and the booty of the Spanish Main, to knowledge as with Magellan and the careful, coast-charting Captain Cook.

But in the accounts of their lives and adventures, somehow, the sea and its power have been diminished a little. Not the sea, but men at sea hold the focus, and the waters travelled become a form of difficult and dangerous terrain, something less than the mysterious, moving entity so necessary to our lives.

Who has written greatly of the sea? You will all have in mind one or another author who has written compelling narratives of adventure at sea. Among modern authors, Richard Henry Dana, Jack London, Sterling Hayden, C. S. Forester, Richard Hughes, Ernest Hemingway, Herman Wouk, Nicholas Monserrat, Patrick O'Brian come quickly to mind. But my thought is of another kind of writer, one with the skill to move an account of man's maritime adventuring into another dimension—not the authors of sea stories where men and storms huff and fight at one another, but stories or poems or dramas wherein men and the sea come into the kind of relationship that might be called mythic—accounts that are at heart philosophical or theological narratives and that explore the fundamental way man and the sea have belonged together from the first syllable of recorded time. There are not many such. Indeed, surprisingly few, in English at least, have spoken of the sea in this way.

My own list of such writers is short, partly because, after Homer, I speak only of English-speaking authors: Shakespeare toward the end of his life, Coleridge, Melville, Conrad, and Eugene O'Neill. It is a special list of poets and moralists who, looking deep into the sea, have looked into themselves.

I have not time this afternoon to explore this matter in any detail, but perhaps a few brief quotations will at least suggest my meaning:

From Melville:

Heaved and heaved, still unrestingly heaved the black sea, as if its tides were a conscience; and the great mundane soul were in anguish and remorse for the long sin and suffering it had bred.

From Conrad:

The problems of life [on the *Narcissus*] seemed too voluminous for the narrow limits of human speech, and by common consent it was abandoned to the great sea that had from the beginning enfolded it in its immense grip; to the sea that knew all, and would infallibly unveil to each the wisdom hidden in all errors, the certitude that lurks in doubts, the realm of safety and peace beyond the frontiers of sorrow and fear.

From O'Neill (in a self-portrait as he was before he became a playwright):

When I was on the Squarehead square rigger, bound for Buenos Aires. Full moon in the Trades. The old hooker driving fourteen knots. I lay on the bowsprit, facing astern, with the waters foaming into spume under me, the masts with every sail white in the moonlight, towering high above me. I became drunk with the beauty and singing rhythm of it, and for a moment I lost myself—actually lost my life. I was set free! I dissolved in the sea, became white sails and flying spray, became beauty and rhythm, became moonlight and the ship and the high dim-starred sky! I belonged without past or future, within peace and unity and a wild joy, within something greater than my own life, or the life of Man, to Life itself! To God, if you want to put it that way.

Such views of the sea as dynamic and directly concerned with the affairs of mortals are at some remove from the aspects of the sea as it plays a scenic role in adventure stories. This is the sea that is a power, a center, a governor and a need. Conrad calls the crew of the *Narcissus* "the everlasting children of the mysterious sea," and therewith makes the sea into a kind of mothering force controlling the generations of seamen who come to her. With this, O'Neill, who at the beginning of his career was heavily influenced by Conrad's work, is in full agreement.

When he began to write, O'Neill came under the influence of European expressionist dramatists who were painfully exploring the agony of little men crumbling under the pressure of forces over which they had no control. His first publication in the amateurish collection *Thirst and Other One-Act Plays* gives several examples of what he came to consider the action of "ironic fate" on the lives of his characters. Quite often he was ready to accept maladroit, O. Henry-like plotting as evidence of "fate" at work, but even then, he revealed a concern for something more than the ordinary turns of coincidence that characterized the short stories and vaudeville sketches of this century's second decade. He appears to have felt that behind the affairs of men and women a powerful, implacable awareness was at work, making human action dismally ironic. The nature of the force and its relationship to the characters was not a matter he could readily define. In the title play, *Thirst,* (A Mulatto Sailor, A Wealthy Man and a Peasant Woman adrift on a raft surrounded by sharks) the parching sun looks down "Like a great angry eye of God," and in a companion piece, *Fog,* (A Poet, a Business Man and a Peasant Woman adrift next to a fog-bound iceberg) "A menacing silence, like the genius of the fog, broods over everything." The sense of something large, aware, omnipotent is there, but imagery is all that is offered as exploration of the force that controls the lives of the characters. It is poetic personification; nothing emerges in the action.

As he matured and gained abler control of his craft, the concern for the nature of the unseen power became more fully articulated, Four short plays concerning the crew of the tramp steamer S. S. *Glencairn,* centered in an exploration of the sea's relationship with the sailors. In the first-written of these, *Bound East for Cardiff,* Yank and Driscoll have planned to leave the sea and find a place on land. But Yank is injured, and any hope of reaching port to get medical aid is dashed by a fog which surrounds the ship, slowing its progress fatally for the injured man. As Yank dies he sees an apparition—"A pretty lady dressed in black"—who comes into the forecastle and seems to welcome and receive him. No explanation is offered, but the mourning woman must be associated with the sea. In sum, the play suggests that most sailors are bound to the sea, and that apostasy such as Yank and Driscoll plan—leaving the sea—is an offense the sea will punish. The imprisoning fog lifts as Yank dies. Yet as the image of the pretty lady suggests, the sea is kind and, in the end, will receive its children gently and mourn for them.

The depiction of men bound to the sea is fully realized in the best of the *Glencairn* plays, *The Moon of the Caribbees.* The freighter is anchored off a West Indian island. A native chant—monotonous and unceasing—is heard from the shore. The sailors, restless and a little randy, await the arrival of some bumboat women bringing them rum and sex. The music irritates them, the moonlight falls over them like a bright net, and when the women arrive, they move exuberantly into the forecastle. One man, an alien at sea, laments what he has lost on land. The bacchanal in the forecastle erupts in a fight. Then silence closes around the ship and all that is heard is the chant, all that is seen is the moonlight on the calm water. The play is as close as drama comes to a pure poem. Nothing happens. The only real action in the work is the conflict between the men and the chant, which reminds them that they are what O'Neill called the "Sea Mother's sons," and that they belong to her. The play is a depiction of men fixed where they belong, where no act of will intrudes to draw them away from the encompassing power of the sea.

O'Neill's first successful long play, *Beyond the Horizon,* continued the exploration of man's "belonging" to a force that was to be felt in nature. Now, however, he brought the land into the picture and gave it a proprietary power equivalent to that he had earlier attributed only to the sea. The play concerns two brothers, Robert and Andrew Mayo, who live on a small New England farm. Robert, however, yearns for the sea. To travel beyond the horizon is his dream and his right destiny. Andrew, on the other hand, is the land's man, a true farmer, to whom the earth responds. A triangular love affair distorts the right relationship, so that Andrew goes to sea and Robert stays to manage the farm. Both men are destroyed; the earth rejects Robert and the sea corrupts Andrew. The mysterious, god-like force in earth and sea is now clearly defined, and O'Neill's first major theme can be strongly set forth: the need men have to belong to such a force.

After *Beyond the Horizon,* O'Neill's next statement of the theme was to be *"Anna Christie"* but the play in its first version was less clearly outlined around the thematic concept. In the winter of 1918, he was in a state of artistic doldrums, waiting for *Beyond the Horizon* to go into production, living at the home of his in-laws and writing little. He read *The Saturday Evening Post* from cover to cover, and certainly his attention was caught by the stories of Peter B. Kyne and others who specialized in tales of nautical derring-do. Out of this came *Chris Christophersen,* the first version of *"Anna Christie,"* which told a complex story of Chris's barge being rammed by a freighter and of the romance between Anna and the freighter's second mate as they voyage through moonlit nights to Buenos Aires. The narrative is improbable, and the characters are cardboard. The young Lynn Fontanne played Anna as a decorous British typist who refreshes herself from the fatigues of an Atlantic crossing with a cup of tea. Her lover is a pale non-entity who is content with being second mate because there is little work and no responsibility in the job. The play—in which O'Neill appeared to have lost interest by the time of its production—was worthy of its failure.

In rewriting it, O'Neill came to the most complete statement he had yet expressed of the theme of belonging. Anna's story, like that of the Mayo brothers in *Beyond the Horizon* has something of the narrative simplicity of a fable. Anna, sent from her right habitat, the sea, is nearly destroyed in the alien environment of the land. Menial servitude, prostitution, and incipient tuberculosis are her fate on land. Coming to the sea, her life changes. The fog surrounds her softly and makes her feel clean: "It's like I'd come home," she says. "I feel...'s if this was the right place for me to fit in.... I feel clean...I feel happy." She adds, in reply to her father's foreboding words, that if something bad happens it will be "Gawd's will." Chris cries in fierce protest, "No! Dat ole davil, sea, she ain't God!" At this point the voice of Mat Burke is heard calling from the sea, and Anna's destiny is determined.

Anna's two men also have a fabular significance about them. Mat has something of the sea's strength in him, capable of rowing for two days to bring the survivors of the wrecked ship's crew to safety, contemptuous of the land ("Digging spuds in the muck from dawn to dark?... I wasn't made for it."), and unafraid of a quick, clean death by drowning. Anna's father, once a bo'sun, tried to turn his back on the sea, but has been unable to make the cut completely. Now, on his coal barge hugging the shoreline, neither land's man nor sea's man, he lives a crustacean existence avoiding the deep waters he once knew.

The three are the sea's people, and the play shows unequivocally that the strong force of the sea, be it God or "ole Davil," intends no harm to those who belong to it. For all O'Neill's fussing about the happy ending of the play, no other ending was possible in the poetic and philosophical thematic structure.

The writing of *"Anna Christie"* brought O'Neill to the edge of clarification of the meaning of his sensibility about the sea. As the play went into production in November, 1921, O'Neill began work on *The Hairy Ape,* in which the need to belong was dramatized as the agony of Yank, the brute-like stoker on a trans-Atlantic liner. Yank has many qualities in common with Mat Burke, but a love of the sea is not one of them. Instead, Yank believes in the force embodied in steel:

I'm de ting in coal dat makes it boin; I'm steam and oil for de engines; I'm de ting in noise dat makes yuh hear it; I'm smoke and express trains and steamers and factory whistles; I'm de ting in gold dat makes it money! And I'm what makes iron into steel! Steel, dat stands for de whole ting! And I'm steel—steel—steel!

His creed is shouted to drown out the reminiscence of an old sailor, Paddy, who recalls in words not unlike those of Edmund Tyrone in *Long Day's Journey into Night,* the romantic days of the sailing ships:

Nights and days! Nights when the foam of the wake would be flaming wid fire, when the sky'd be blazing and winking wid stars. Or the full of the moon maybe. Then you'd see her driving through the gray night, her sails stretching aloft all silver and white, not a sound on the deck, the lot of us dreaming dreams.... 'Twas them days men belonged to ships, not now. 'Twas them days a ship was part of the sea, and a man was part of a ship, and the sea joined all together and made it one.

To follow were other considerations of "belonging"—*The Fountain, Desire Under the Elms, The Great God Brown, Strange Interlude,* and one of his most under-rated plays, *Lazarus Laughed.* In all of these, and in other less interesting explorations, O'Neill's characters, and by inference from the constantly recurring inquiry, O'Neill himself, were questing the nature of a god to whom they could belong.

With the writing of *Mourning Becomes Electra,* O'Neill approached the end of the quest for belonging. His modern version of the Electra story eliminated any suggestion of the controlling gods of the Greek legend. Now the controls lie only in the hands of the men and women who must live under what seems like an ancestral curse brought on the house by their own actions. Now, for the first time in his plays, the conscious will controls destiny and the results for his playwriting are important. The sea is lost. Its blessing becomes a memory, a dream, an unrealizable desire, echoing through the play in the chanty song "Shenandoah," which O'Neill said held in it the "brooding rhythm of the sea."

The major work to come, the Tao House plays including the Cycle, *A Tale of Possessors, Self-dispossessed,* had little room for the mysterious, empowering sea. Even the cycle play laid on shipboard, *The Calms of Capricorn,* views the sea as an antagonist to be beaten by man's will. I find it a matter of interest and concern that in *The Iceman Cometh* no one of the men at Harry Hope's saloon has any connection with the sea. At the last, O'Neill turned his back on the sea, not to look at the land, but to look within himself, and to explore the memory of his family he found there. Then in Edmund Tyrone's words, the sea and the beauty of belonging was brought back as a poetic memory, which Edmund calls "a saint's vision of beatitude." But it is only a memory. For those locked in that tragic world memory can bring surcease for a time, but it can no longer provide the soul's salvation it brought to Anna Christie.

Children of the Sea: *The Moon of the Caribbees*

A tramp freighter, the S. S. *Glencairn,* anchored off a Caribbean island. A native chant circulating endlessly through the tropical night. The full moon, the moon of the Caribbees, wrapping the freighter and its crew in a cocoon of light.

Nothing important happens; nothing can happen to the men in the freighter's crew, who, without realizing it, are possessed and protected by the sea as if they were the sea's children.

Eugene O'Neill wrote *The Moon of the Caribbees* in 1917. It was the last of four plays he devoted to the crew of the S.S. *Glencairn,* a ship very like the one he had sailed on in his seafaring days before he found his destiny as a playwright.

Late in his life, he would describe his writing as "faithful realism," but *The Moon of the Caribbees* is more than that. The sailors, speaking a babel of dialects, are modeled on men he had sailed with, and the details of the ship and the nautical procedures are accurately depicted. Yet for the young O'Neill, impatient with the general run of plays he saw and ambitious to become a poet of the theatre, it was not enough to show only what was there to be seen. Realistic action must be made remarkable by showing its place in some large philosophical or religious scheme. Only then, he felt, could a play approach poetry.

In the theatre of 1917, melodramatic confrontations, stories that depended on sudden surprises and stale dramatic tricks were the order of the day. There is nothing of such tired plotting in O'Neill's play. The sailors *do* nothing; they simply *are.* They want nothing they cannot have. No one hungers, no one plots. The moonlit deck where they walk is all the world.

Their simplicity provides the means for extending the play beyond its surface realism. Perhaps because of some genetic element in their nature, the sailors belong to the sea. They move as the sea moves in a lifetime of ebb and flow, in unity with the ship and its element.

As O'Neill was to express the idea a little later, "A ship was part of the sea, and man was a part of a ship, and the sea joined all together and made it one." For the sailors, unthinking acquiescence to the powerful, natural and god-like force of the sea is the only way of life.

The binding of crew, ship and sea is dramatized by the chant heard from the nearby island. The sound, drifting over the water is continuous and unvaryingly monotonous, but like the sea and the moonlight, it *is*—a part of the great natural harmony in which the men have their meaning.

They hear it and are troubled by it. It reminds them that they are like enchanted men, unable to exert their wills. They fight it, and try to drown it out by singing sea chanties and reveling noisily in the fo'c'sle.

But the chant is not to be stopped. It reiterates the sailors' truth, saying: "You are the sea's children. The sea's will is your will. Your destiny is what the sea brings you. Do not seek to act; do not seek to possess; let yourself be possessed—by the sea, by the moonlight. In this lies your content."

Although the men in a reflex action fight against the implications, no heresy to the god-force of the sea is possible. The chant prevails until, as O'Neill writes in his final stage direction, it becomes *"the mood of the moonlight made audible."*

Children of the Sea: *Bound East for Cardiff*

In *Bound East for Cardiff,* Eugene O'Neill spoke for the first time in his authentic voice. He wrote the play in 1914, as he began his career. Alone among several unplayable efforts, this play signalled the direction he was to follow. Perhaps because it made use of his experiences on a tramp freighter like the S. S. *Glencairn,* the play gained a truth his other early efforts lacked.

Coincidentally, but appropriately, it became the first play to herald the arrival of a new movement in theatre—the twentieth century American theatre that O'Neill would soon dominate.

In those days, Provincetown on the sea-surrounded tip of Cape Cod was a summer retreat for young artists from New York City. In 1916, among other summer games, a group of them determined to put on a play. They created a theatre from a shed built out on a wharf, through whose planking the tidal waters could be heard and seen.

Eagerly they canvassed the village for writers who could supply them with plays, and in their search came upon O'Neill who was living far from town in a shack among the sand dunes. One night he shyly brought them his sea play and waited in an adjoining room while they read and debated its value.

It was an important moment. There was little debate about the value of what they had heard. As one of the group later said, "Then we knew what we were for." What O'Neill had brought them was a new kind of drama, one that did not depend on tricky plots or exotic locales which were the improbable actions of the escapist romances regularly offered on Broadway.

The first night of the play entered theatrical legend. As in the play, the fog was thick, surrounding the wharf, and the sea—so important to O'Neill—lapped at the pilings under the floor. On the makeshift stage, there came into being a new kind of truth—O'Neill's truth—and a blending of reality and poetry new to American stages.

That Fall, the players moved to Greenwich Village in New York City, organized themselves as "The Provincetown Players," and committed themselves to presenting the work of new American playwrights. From this nucleus, actors, designers, directors and playwrights were to emerge with a dedication to a modern art of the theatre.

The play that started it all was deceptively simple: two men speaking in a grimy fo'c'sle, confessing to one another an unexpressed dream that had lain at the center of their friendship, a dream of some day leaving the sea to live on the land.

It is a situation that later writers as different as John Steinbeck and Edward Albee were to find compelling. Were it not that O'Neill felt the sea to have a god-like control over men and therefore did not find the universe empty, the play might be held to resemble the existentialist dramas of writers like Beckett and Sartre.

As O'Neill has it, the sailors belong to the sea. Any dream of renouncing the sea for the land is a kind of betrayal, and the sea punishes their apostasy. Yank's lungs are crushed in an accident and the sea brings in the dense fog so that the *Glencairn* cannot carry him with speed to shore. Yank therefore must die and the friendship end.

Then, as a mother forgives her children, the sea sends the dying man a vision of "a pretty lady dressed in black" to comfort him and to mourn for him. The play's first title was "Children of the Sea."

Bound East for Cardiff is a gentle play, but it is an impressive depiction of human loneliness and need. It stands as a fitting prelude to the American theatre about to be born.

Children of the Sea: *In the Zone*

In the Zone, written during the first World War in 1917, reflects the newly discovered horror of submarine warfare. Its timeliness made it Eugene O'Neill's first popular success. After its initial production in Greenwich Village it was purchased by a commercial manager and played into 1918 on a vaudeville circuit. In Canada and England, it gave the young actor Raymond Massey his first opportunity on stage.

The royalties it brought were welcome and enabled O'Neill to marry, but the play's success, paradoxically, made the playwright doubt the worth of his work. "Is it," he asked himself, "only a commercial melodrama?"

Certainly the play has elements of melodrama lacking in the other *Glencairn* plays. The submarine-haunted sea that breeds tension in the men, the suspicious Smitty and his hidden black box that may be a bomb, the furtive spying, the trap, the capture—these are all melodramatic. Compared with *The Moon of the Caribbees* and *Bound East for Cardiff, In the Zone* is suspenseful in the easiest theatrical way, depending on surprise and an unexpected, sentimental resolution.

No doubt these elements made it attractive to war-time audiences in vaudeville theatres. If it had offered no more, O'Neill might well have collected his royalties and forgotten the play's existence, once its tour ended.

But the play in the context of the *Glencairn* cycle adds something important to the philosophical picture of the sailors' relation to the sea. The other plays show how some men are the sea's children and find in its power a life-long nurturing good. Unthinkingly, they belong, and without exertion of their wills are brought into harmony with the natural rhythms of the element.

In *The Moon of the Caribbees* the kinship of the sailors to one another and to the sea seems more important than their individuality.

Their identity comes from the fact that they belong—to the sea and the ship and the crew. Only Smitty, sitting apart and hating the moonlight and the native chant, does not join in their revelry. In the harmony of man and ship and sea, he is discordant, an alien who does not belong.

The character of the man who does not belong was to become a central figure in O'Neill's dramatic scheme. In later plays, he will be shown as a quester after some vaguely defined salvation that will protect him as the sea protects the crew, and that will bring him a sense of beatitude. He will become the man with the touch of a poet—who has a glimmering vision into an ultimate truth, who feels with pain man's need to belong to a god, but who, because he cannot see the whole truth, is doomed to wander as if he were astray on a timeless foggy night—questing, never finding.

Smitty is not this figure, but he is O'Neill's first sketch of such a man. What he will come to mean to O'Neill can be surmised by the fact that in plays written shortly after *In the Zone,* O'Neill will describe his appearance so as to suggest his own face. For O'Neill, he will become a self-portrait.

Here, the full meaning of the character is submerged in melodrama, but Smitty marks the first exploration of an important creative development in O'Neill's philosophy.

Children of the Sea: *The Long Voyage Home*

In European and American literature of the late nineteenth and early twentieth centuries, a dark view of man's destiny often prevailed. In a world that had been shaken by Darwin's theory of evolution, Freud's exploration of man's inner self, and the tragic philosophy of Friedrich Nietzsche, writers became increasingly aware that men were not positioned at the center of a benevolent universe, and that their small acts of will had little effect on the course of the world in time.

In their poems, novels and plays, these writers asserted that men were the victims of energies they could not control. Both through forces of heredity and environment, they became the doomed playthings of a meaningless, insensate and often ironic fate. They had no recourse but to progress toward an unheroic destiny. Unlike the fated protagonists of Greek drama, they had no god on whom they could lay their burdens. No divinity, possessed of a concerned mind and capable of pitying or punishing, existed beyond their doomed selves.

As a young man, Eugene O'Neill read, admired and often imitated many of these somber writers, particularly Stephen Crane, Theodore Dreiser, Frank Norris, Jack London and Joseph Conrad.

He could not, however, accept the world as so pitiless and godless a place as some of them had done. He had been first educated in a Catholic boy's academy, and, although he did not follow the faith of his parents as an adult, he did not lose the sense that man needs a god to make his life meaningful. He knew by heart and often recited the poem by Francis Thompson, "The Hound of Heaven," in which the poet, pursued by the great hound of God, runs in fear from his salvation. Some lines of the poem show O'Neill's feeling:

I fled Him, down the nights and down the days;
    I fled Him, down the arches of the years;
I fled Him, down the labyrinthine ways
    Of my own mind; and in the midst of tears
I hid from Him, and under running laughter.
    Up vistaed hopes I sped;
    And shot precipitated
Adown Titanic glooms of chasmed fears
    From those strong Feet that followed, followed after.
    But with unhurrying chase
    And unperturbed pace,
Deliberate speed, majestic instancy,
    They beat—and a Voice beat
    More instant than the Feet—
"All things betray thee, who betrayest Me."

The paradox of O'Neill's life—implicit in much of his mature writing—is that like the fugitive in the poem, he ran in flight not away from but toward a belief that would make the modern world less stark, drab, cruel and chill with irony.

As a beginning writer. he called on memories of the sea and felt that some men had in their nature a quality that responded devoutly to the sea's power. What these men were caused them to respond to it, and the great sea had, in consequence, a god-like control of their destinies. For the young O'Neill, to view the sea as such a force made the world appear less empty than other writers had found it.

But O'Neill was a "modern." Simply to believe was somehow to turn "soft," and so he set himself to show that the god-like sea could punish those who set their individual wills against its own. The sea, like the hound of heaven, could pursue.

Thus it is that Yank in *Bound East for Cardiff* is punished for dreaming of living on land, and, in *The Long Voyage Home,* that Olson's attempt to return to his farm and family meets an end which—in the context of the cycle—must be seen as the result of the sea's power to deal with those who sin against it.

O'Neill draws no specific moral from his small story, and like the writers he admired and to an extent emulated, he lets Olson go to his end on the death ship with no lamentation. Only in the larger context which the four plays together provide can Olson's "ironic fate" be seen as his punishment for pitting his will against the power of the sea.

About *The Emperor Jones*

Once the Provincetown Players were situated in New York City, plays by O'Neill became a staple of their offerings. He wrote twelve one-act plays for them, and on their inadequate stage, he learned the essentials of a playwright's craft. His work was hard-edged and daring and sufficiently avant-garde to interest arbiters of new twentieth century literature, notably George Jean Nathan and H. L. Mencken, who published three of the plays in their magazine *The Smart Set*.

The one-act plays were the basis of his reputation, but although they foreshadowed a new style of American playwriting, they were not major works of dramatic art. O'Neill still ranked with the Village amateurs, a long distance off Broadway.

The change from amateur to professional, when it came, was rapid. In 1920, he first appeared on Broadway under professional management with the four-act tragedy *Beyond the Horizon*. The play was hesitantly introduced in a series of "special matinees" with a cast recruited from other Broadway productions. It was received with enthusiasm and soon went into a regular run, winning the first of O'Neill's four Pulitzer Prizes. A second try for fully professional acceptance, a sea play, *Chris Christophersen*, failed out of town and was not seen until with radical revision it came to Broadway in 1921 as *"Anna Christie"* and won his second Pulitzer Prize.

Between these two successes, at the Provincetown Playhouse in the fall of 1920, O'Neill offered a play that more than any other was to cement his reputation as a daringly unconventional, thrilling and fully professional dramatist.

The Emperor Jones was not cut to ordinary theatrical patterns nor was it an easy play to produce. In the small confines of the Provincetown Playhouse stage, the Players' director, George Cram

Cook, built an innovative scenic element, a plaster dome, modeled after a German development, against whose white, unwrinkled concavity, light could move in such a way as to cast the action into chiaroscuro. To build the dome required the entirety of the Playhouse's treasure—all $360.00 of it—but Cook's certainty that the play could not be staged without it was an important commitment to the play's ultimate success.

More important was the casting of the Emperor. O'Neill understood that no white actor in blackface could touch the character. The search for a black actor capable of the role ended when the Players found Charles S. Gilpin running an elevator at Macy's department store. Gilpin had had some stage experience in Harlem stock companies, vaudeville and minstrel shows. He brought to the role of the Emperor unexpected qualities that the dramatist Moss Hart described as "inner violence and maniacal power." Throughout his life, O'Neill maintained that no other actor had so fully realized all aspects of any character he had created as had Gilpin.

The production made Gilpin an overnight star, but the strain told, and he began to drink and to alter the dialogue during performance. When the play was given a London production, Gilpin was replaced by the young Paul Robeson. Rejected, Gilpin said, "I created the role of the Emperor. That role belongs to me. That Irishman, he just wrote the play."

Gilpin was without question right that the role was his. Outside of a few short plays for Harlem theatres, Brutus Jones was the first significant role written for a black actor that was more than a Stepin Fetchit sketch. Jones is a fully developed character, sustained at the core of the central action and heroic in its dimensions. Possibly marred for today's audiences by its stereotypical view of black history, the play still offers a powerful characterization of a tragic human being with no touch of condescension. Gilpin's performance in the role O'Neill provided for him was a breakthrough in the progress of the black in theatre.

The play was a startling success. The first-night audience cheered and stayed in the theatre for so long that Cook was reduced to striking the set and showing off the scenic capabilities of the new dome. The next day, lines forming around the block from the box office signalled that the happy days of the Provincetown amateurs were finished. From then on, the expectation of audiences and critics was that the Players must become professionals or perish. *The Emperor Jones* moved to Broadway, but the Players could not capitalize on their success, and the Playhouse shortly came under a different management that was less amateur and to some extent less free.

That *The Emperor Jones* appeared in 1920 was not, perhaps, entirely an accident. The years following World War I were to see a new energy in American arts and letters. In 1920, T. S. Eliot's *Poems,* Sinclair Lewis's *Main Street,* and F. Scott Fitzgerald's *This Side of Paradise* appeared as heralds of things to come. New styles, new commitments—the new energies that were to make the Twenties "roar"—were providing the yeast for new enthusiasms. The success of *The Emperor Jones* placed it firmly with what was modern in the large literary scene and it set a new mark for the theatre of the moment. Essentially a long monologue between two framing scenes, the excitement generated by the increasing panic of the hero, reinforced by the accelerating pulse of the native drums heard throughout the central action, pointed a direction that the theatre could take toward an imaginative new artistry in design and performance, and a new seriousness in the exploration of important themes.

The importance of the play's theme today may be debatable. O'Neill followed the lead of a number of writers of the earlier years of the century, especially Jack London and Frank Norris, in exploring what might be called a post-Darwinian concept of "reverse evolution." London in *The Call of the Wild* had traced the "devolution" of the dog Buck to his primitive roots as a beast of prey, while Norris had explored a similar concept in a human being in *Vandover and the Brute.* Jones's return through scenes of his racial history to his jungle roots and the crocodile god that possesses him follows the same narrative line.

O'Neill offered many mundane explanations for the source of the play. The drums, he said, were suggested by his memory of the pulsing of his blood when he became ill with malaria fever while on a gold-prospecting expedition in Honduras. The character of the Emperor, he claimed, was derived from a number of West Indian potentates, a former president of Haiti, Vilbrun Guillaume Sam, who boasted that only a silver bullet could kill him, the revolutionary Toussaint L'Ouverture, and the Haitian emperor Henri Christophe who committed suicide with a silver bullet. O'Neill's jungle may have had precedents in those of Joseph Conrad's *The Heart of Darkness* and Vachel Lindsay's poem "The Congo." In the panic-stricken flight through a wilderness that becomes a search for the fugitive's self, *The Emperor Jones* is reminiscent in its dramatic rhythm and in many specific details of the second act of Henrik Ibsen's *Peer Gynt*. The play's contention that a man belongs to a jealous god—in Jones's case the dark god of the jungle whose power he futilely tries to deny with his silver bullet—is a theme that O'Neill had developed before in his early sea plays, where he held the sea to be a possessive god, and to which he would soon return in his next work, *The Hairy Ape*, where the protagonist, like Jones, must follow a path of reverse evolution to find in the figure of a great ape, the embodiment of the force to which he belongs.

Yet when O'Neill's debts are acknowledged and the major sources of the play noted, *The Emperor Jones* is a work of unusual originality and power, in its own time the source of a fine film and a distinguished opera. It marked O'Neill's turn from the uncertainty of amateurism to the full control of his artistry as a professional playwright. Even yet, *The Emperor Jones* is able to excite and deeply move an audience.

Children of the Sea:
Little Orphan *"Anna Christie"*

By 1920, the young Eugene O'Neill was feeling his oats. Production of his one-act sea plays by small theatre companies in Greenwich Village and the publication of several in avant-garde magazines had marked him as a serious and experimental playwright. In the hands of a Broadway producer, George C. Tyler, his *Beyond the Horizon* was a substantial critical success and won his first Pulitzer Prize. To follow the rural tragedy, he offered a drama different in tone and form: a sea play, *Chris Christophersen,* called for short, *Chris.*

Like many of his one-act plays, *Chris* was based on characters and events he had known at sea and in his derelict days at New York waterfront saloons. Christophersen's original was a barge captain, an old Swede who had once been a deep-water sailor, but who had, in the sailor's phrase, "swallowed the anchor" and given up the rigors of life at sea. Now he spent his time on his barge or in Jimmy-the-Priest's saloon, drinking and razzing the sea as an "ole davil" who held nothing but ill-will toward sailors. One freezing night, he fell from his barge and drowned. O'Neill would have seen this accident as *Chris's* "ironic fate," an example of the sea's power to control the destinies of those who sailed upon it.

Testimony to the sea's power over men had formed the thematic center of the four one-act plays set on the S. S. *Glencairn.* Unthinking and undemanding, the Glencairn sailors lived as the sea dictated. Any attempt to leave the sea or to deny its power was heretical and sometimes resulted in fatal punishment. However, if the sailors accepted the

Program note for the Longwharf Theatre Production of "Anna Christie," New Haven, Connecticut, March, 1990.

sea's design without seeking a different destiny, they entered into harmony with its force as part of a great immensity of being. As O'Neill put it, they "belonged."

Chris, however, had denied the sea and rejected the destiny it held for him. Crawling between land and deep water, he was an apostate who became the victim of the sea's power and who was forced to suffer the ironic fate in store for him. His life and death would have made a satisfactory one-act mood piece like the *Glencairn* plays, but as O'Neill, trying to work in larger forms, expanded the story into three acts, the play became something quite different.

Chris tells of the old sea captain whose daughter (played in the first version by Lynn Fontanne) has been respectably brought up in England. She has in mind a career as a secretary, but she accepts a vacation trip on her father's barge. The barge is rammed by a steamer bound for South America, and she and her father are taken aboard. There she meets and falls in love with the handsome second mate. Although Chris is enraged that she plans to marry a sailor and melodramatically tries to stab her lover, the play ends happily with Chris accepting the position of bo'sun on the steamer, while the mate studies to become a captain so that he may take his bride with him on his voyages.

Somewhere, evidently, the play slipped its moorings. It closed out of town, but its failure seemed not to matter to O'Neill, who came to realize that the play was forced and not up to his philosophic, poetic or dramatic potential.

Young in his career, he was not entirely certain what his standards were. Yet, in *Beyond the Horizon* he had developed the theme of "belonging" into a tragedy of the brothers Mayo, one a child of the sea who deserts the sea, the other an apostate man of the land. The concept that men belong by something in their nature to a force greater than they are, and to which they owe unthinking, complete allegiance was to be set forth more explicitly in *The Hairy Ape* (1922) and to receive its most careful exposition in *Desire Under the Elms* (1924). However the theme was touched only cursorily in *Chris*, and as O'Neill clarified his aims, it was not long before he was rethinking the play, and turning Anna from typist to trollop. Old Chris had held his own as the central figure of the first version, but with the advent of the new Anna, he was forced from center stage to make room for her and her new lover, the powerful stoker Mat Burke. Anna's story now conveyed a philosophical implication not to be found in the first draft of her character. As O'Neill came to view her, she was the sea's true daughter. Her father's hatred of the sea had led him to send her inland to be raised on a farm, but her sojourn on the land separated her disastrously from her rightful place. Like the brothers in *Beyond the Horizon*, she was unable to survive in an alien world. Tuberculosis and prostitution marked her for a sour, short, despairing life. Her return to her father brought her to the sea where she was no longer alien but could find redemption and salvation.

Her father, nervous at her grateful response to the sea, tells her that he was a fool to bring her to the sea on his barge, but she replies that whatever happens will be God's will. Chris is roused to protest, crying: "No! Dat ole davil sea she ain't God!" In the silence following his outburst, a voice from the water is heard and shortly Anna receives her welcoming gift from the sea, the exhausted, ship-wrecked Mat Burke.

The story thereafter moves to its logical end in O'Neill's demonstration that the sea will determine the fates of all three. Mat, whose physical power is allied to the strength of the sea, is Anna's destined lover, and although for a time the values of the shore threaten their relationship, Anna's honesty and Mat's ability to receive her as the sea has, bring the lovers to harmony in the end.

Other endings were possible. A gun makes its appearance during the last act, and it was used in the first Berlin production to enable Anna to commit suicide in a paroxysm of guilt. Such an ending, however, was only one more dreary illustration of the wages of sin. O'Neill's trust in the sea's power to cleanse and redeem was stronger than his interest in moralistic castigation of vice. Although Chris carries on about the "ole davil" that has led him and Mat to sign on to the same ship, his words have no more authority than those of any grumbling oldster. The play's action has demonstrated that the sea can only bring blessing.

Which is where the trouble started.

The play, starring the great Pauline Lord, was produced by Arthur Hopkins and sensitively designed by Robert Edmond Jones. O'Neill said that it was "one of the best acted I have ever seen, and the best set." The reception was favorable, but the play's ending in the prospect of marital bliss bothered a number of high-toned critics. Although he was a life-long friend and supporter of O'Neill, the critic George Jean Nathan pounced on the ending as being a typical Broadway commercial compromise—a happy ending, unworthy of so promising and daring a playwright.

To fight what he called the suggestion of "a Henry Arthur Jones compromise" in the ending, O'Neill wrote a letter to *The New York Times* explaining his intention:

It would have been so easy...to have made my last act a tragic one.... But looking deep into the hearts of my people, I saw it couldn't be done. It would not have been true.... They would act in just the silly, immature, compromising way that I have made them act,...a bit tragically humorous in vacillating weakness.

To Nathan he wrote "The happy ending is merely the comma at the end of a gaudy introductory clause, with the body of the sentence still unwritten. (In fact I once thought of calling the play 'Comma')"

But the punctuation of a play at the final curtain is a full stop, and a playgoer leaving the theatre may be forgiven for being content that Anna got her Mat and that Chris is back at sea where he belongs. Conventional theatrical formulas have their way with the best laid philosophical schemes. Consider the refusal of the public to permit Eliza Doolittle to marry Freddy as a parallel example.

O'Neill, however, was stubborn and twisted and turned in his attempt to make the ending darker than it was. "There is no ending ... at all," he wrote, "either happy or unhappy.... A naturalistic play is life. Life doesn't end." And again: "That last act is [the doing of Anna, Mat and Chris].... I told them they ought to die rather than give in to such weakness. But they were stubbornly resolved. They even insisted their last pitiful groping has a deep significance." And later: " I don't choose to write naturalistic *'Anna Christies'* all my life. I consider it the least worthy of my plays with one possible exception—though I think the last act, which was so criticized as conventional, was the most courageous and original act of the play."

What in fact had happened was that O'Neill had evolved his theme of belonging to its logical end. Happiness—or at least harmony—lies in submission to the sea, and though life on the sea may lead to the clean quick death by drowning Mat speaks of, this is a better way of being for the sea's children than anything on land. Thus the play was anchored in the possibility of harmony between men and women and their guiding force, and it became in the broadest sense of the term a romantic comedy.

The play was well received in New York and on tour; its successful London production formed the beginning of O'Neill's European reputation. In 1923, Blanche Sweet starred in an excellent silent film, and seven years later it served to introduce the great Greta Garbo to talking pictures. "GARBO TALKS!" the publicity shouted, and nervous fans the world over waited to see if the most alluring of silent actresses would be able to make the transition to sound. O'Neill had written what became a perfect entrance for her as she slouched into Johnny-the-Priest's saloon wearing an unforgettable Adrian hat and rasped her first words: "Gimme a whiskey—ginger ale on the side. And don't be stingy, baby." There was no difficulty thereafter for Miss Garbo's vocal glamor.

For O'Neill, however, the difficulty remained. He continued to hear the carping of the critics, and he did his best to disown the play. Although it had won his second Pulitzer Prize, when a Nobel Prize edition of nine of his plays was being published, he insisted that *"Anna Christie"* be omitted. In later years when he thought of the play, he felt it had only been a vehicle for Lord, and when the young Ingrid Bergman undertook the role, he felt it was being used to "build up" Bergman's new career in America and again disavowed the play and its merits. In short, he did everything he could to orphan *"Anna Christie."* Yet in 1944, writing to Arthur Hopkins after Pauline Lord had appeared in a radio broadcast of the play, he said, "Polly in *"Anna Christie"* again certainly brings back a host of pleasant memories.... There was a spirit then that has been lost. There were uncompromising idealists with real love for what the American theatre might become."

To the sentimental, his words may suggest that finally Anna and O'Neill found their way to a happy ending.

Children of the Sea: *The Hairy Ape*

O'Neill wrote *The Hairy Ape* in 1921, following the success of *The Emperor Jones* the previous year. He wrote it rapidly, and through the agency of the producer Arthur Hopkins, who had staged *"Anna Christie,"* it was moved uptown from the Provincetown Playhouse to became a popular success on Broadway. In the person of Louis Wolheim, the figure of Yank, the Hairy Ape, became a memorable creation in the American theatre.

The play was structured in the same pattern as *The Emperor Jones* in eight short scenes centering on the desperate flight of the central character seeking to discover where he belongs. Yank, like Jones, runs through a kind of wilderness to his eventual destruction by a primitive force. Although it is less exotic than *The Emperor Jones,* the play nevertheless creates a vivid, unusual and unforgettable series of scenes, especially those in the bowels of the ship, with the tumult of sound O'Neill calls for: *"The brazen clang of the furnace doors as they are flung open or slammed shut, the grating, teeth-gritting grind of steel against steel, of crunching coal,...the roar of leaping flames, the monotonous throbbing beat of the engines,"* all built into a rhythm, *"a mechanical regulated recurrence."* The strangeness of the whole is much like the throbbing of the drums that pursue Jones through the jungle, and the play frequently departs from realism to follow the mode of the Expressionistic theatre with its emphasis on abstraction and symbols. Visually, it partakes of some of the aspects of the then popular Constructivist movement in painting.

In the end, however, it is not the visual style, but the energy of the desperate central action that gives the play its force. Yank is the lord of the stokehole: *"broader, fiercer, more truculent, more powerful, more sure of himself than the rest. They respect his superior strength—the grudging respect of fear. Then, too, he represents to them a self-expression, the very last word in what they are, their most highly developed individual."* O'Neill places him on an evolutionary ladder (O'Neill required the actor on stage from time to time to assume the pose of Rodin's stature, "The Thinker," which was designed as the central figure for the sculpture "The Gates of Hell") but he also makes clear that Yank has developed to a stage where he has become the embodiment of the powers that drive contemporary civilization, steam and steel, and as he shouts his capitalistic credo, he asserts the rightness of his life: he "belongs."

Yank was an imaginative recreation of a stoker O'Neill had known in his transatlantic sea-faring days, a strong, tough Irishman named Driscoll. Driscoll appears several times in O'Neill's early plays, under his own name in the *Glencairn* plays, and as Mat Burke in *"Anna Christie."* O'Neill described him as "a giant of a man. He thought a whole lot of himself, was a determined individualist. He was very proud of his strength, his capacity for gruelling work. It seemed to give him mental poise to be able to dominate the stokehole, do more than any of his mates.... He wasn't the type [to] just give up, and he loved life." When he was at sea and later during his vagabond days along the New York waterfront, O'Neill took great pleasure in Driscoll's sustaining friendship. It was therefore a matter of profound concern to him when in 1915, in mid-ocean, Driscoll threw himself overboard. His death was scarring to O'Neill and its inexplicable cause created unanswerable questions. *The Hairy Ape* is as close as O'Neill could come to an understanding of his friend's death.

The narrative of *The Hairy Ape* offers Yank, first, as a creature in harmony with his surroundings, one who, although he is at the bottom, is the personification of the forceful energy of modern civilization. Like the down-and-outs of *The Iceman Cometh*, or the crew of the *Glencairn*, he has no ambition or need. O'Neill frames him between two doctrines, the radical preachings of Long, urging action against the dehumanizing forces of society, and the poetic memories of the beauty of sailing ships expressed by Paddy, which again stresses the dehumanization of man in the present. Although Yank dismisses them with contempt, both views work to make Yank uncertain of his power. Add to these displacing suggestions Mildred's unexpected and intrusive appearance and her hysterical reaction to his strength, which she describes as bestial, and his pride of life is destroyed by doubt. Seeing himself through her eyes, Yank no longer knows what he is. The security of his belonging is gone.

Once he leaves the stokehole, his determination to destroy the gods he has served so well becomes a voyage of self-destruction. Since he is their embodiment, destroying them is a form of suicide. As he begins to think about himself doubt is inevitable and Yank has no place.

In the end, as he meets his death in the embrace of the great ape in the zoo, he recognizes himself in the ape and in dying returns to the primordial force from which he came. Yet O'Neill at the end expresses some doubt even about this. In his last stage direction, he writes, "And perhaps the Hairy Ape at last belongs." There is great uncertainty in the final word, "perhaps."

About *The Iceman Cometh* and *Hughie*

O'Neill wrote the first draft of *The Iceman Cometh* between June 8 and November 26, 1939. In this year, the world fell apart as Poland was invaded and Britain and France declared war on Germany. Throughout the end of the Depression, O'Neill had worked on the Cycle, finishing drafts of *And Give Me Death, The Greed of the Meek* and *More Stately Mansions*. Work on *The Calms of Capricorn* had begun, but the world crisis made it impossible for him to continue his account of the decline and fall of the United States. In the midst of Armageddon, one does not bother to prophesy. O'Neill's reaction to war was predictable. At Tao House, he retreated further into himself than he had ever gone before, as if the only understanding that could come in a world gone mad was the understanding of one's self. The following year he wrote *Hughie* and the scenarios and some draft versions of its companion works in a cycle of one-act plays called *By Way of Obit*. In 1941, he wrote his last completed work, *A Moon for the Misbegotten*. Although he picked at the Cycle, making revisions on *A Touch of the Poet* as late as 1942, the work was at a stalemate. Whatever truths it contained for O'Neill had finally to be explored in another past, his own, and in another way than he had in the Cycle. The last four plays form a network of introspection whose effect is perhaps best expressed in O'Neill's words about *The Iceman Cometh* contained in a letter to Lawrence Langner dated August 11, 1940:

There are moments in it that suddenly strip the secret soul of a man stark naked, not in cruelty or moral superiority, but with an understanding

---

from Travis Bogard, Contour in Time *(N.Y., 1972: Oxford University Press) Reprinted by permission.*

---

compassion which sees him as a victim of the ironies of life and of himself. Those moments are for me the depth of tragedy, with nothing more that can possibly be said.

Compassion produced by a full understanding of man's circumstances and man's essential nature, a compassion which beggars analysis, is O'Neill's final achievement in theatre. The action of each of the four last plays rests in a tale to be told, a tale that is essentially a confession made in hope of absolution. Although the confessional tale is often plotless, often nothing more than a dream, it is a way of reaching out in the dark, of finding pity long denied to old sorrow.

The introspective qualities of the last plays account for their essential lyricism. When *The Iceman Cometh* was first produced in 1946, under the somewhat ponderously reverential conditions that O'Neill's "return" to the New York theatre necessarily occasioned, it brought with it, from producers and reviewers, charges that O'Neill was indulging himself by refusing to cut the work. Langner tells of a time during rehearsals when he timidly reminded O'Neill that the same point had been made eighteen times. O'Neill told him "in a particularly quiet voice, 'I intended it to be repeated eighteen times!'" Although it was obviously not a matter of calculated intention, O'Neill did not indulge in such repetition without full awareness of its theatrical consequences. Like many of his earlier efforts, the repetition not only in *The Iceman Cometh* but in *Long Day's Journey into Night* is essential to the lyric mode of the work, for in these plays O'Neill became the poet he had earlier so often lamented he could not be.

Perhaps the nearest theatrical analogue to *The Iceman Cometh* is Dylan Thomas's *Under Milkwood*. Both are "plays for voices," and the voices are those of the dead, reiterating their stories endlessly in an eternity of silence. Under the circumstances of the play the period slang takes on the special qualities of lyric speech. The movement is musical; the repetition of what is said, often almost without significant development, must be followed as if it were music, as patterned abstraction, implemented through contrapuntal repetitions. It is a kind of "sound effect," but here blended so completely with the action that it becomes the action. There are not many moments in theatre comparable to the canonical weaving of the narratives of betrayal, Hickey's and Parritt's, toward the end of the play. Hickey's long monologue is interspersed by short echoing comments from Parritt telling Larry Slade of his own act of betrayal. Parritt and Hickey do not, really, listen to the words that are said. That is to say, they do not understand one another and from that understanding receive direction. Rather, they move toward the same end without conscious inter-awareness, impelled by purely verbal concatenations, each developing the theme of betrayal as a sound in the air. *The Iceman Cometh* does not need music, yet it should be heard as music is heard with an understanding that it progresses in patterns of sound as much as in patterns of narrative action.

To argue that a play should not be justified by comparison to a musical form has validity. It is, after all, only an analogy, but O'Neill's predilection for Nietzsche would cause him to know that Nietzsche claimed tragedy to have been born from "The Spirit of Music." The lyric movement of the chorus in an Aeschylean or Sophoclean tragedy, *The Coephori* or *Antigone,* for example, is the source of the play's energy, turning as a massive wheel at the center of the narrative, spinning off the tortured action, and giving it life and form. Similarly, *The Iceman Cometh* has a strong choric thrust, developed in lyric repetitions.

The Iceman Cometh is perhaps the most "Greek" of O'Neill's work, built around a central chorus, complete with *choregos* in Harry Hope, and the three principal actors, Hickey, Slade and Parritt. In creating his chorus, O'Neill turned to his memories of time spent in the saloons of lower New York—Jimmy-the-Priest's, the Golden Swan, nicknamed "The Hell-Hole"—and of their inhabitants. Most of the characters are modeled after acquaintances or friends he had observed and whom he placed on stage with special fidelity. Yet, while he is concerned to specify their individuality with affectionate concern, he is also seeking, somewhat in the manner of the Elizabethan "Character" writers, to see in the individual a type. The word "type" occurs frequently in his descriptive stage directions of Hope's roomers: Hugo Kalmar bears *"a strong resemblance to the type of Anarchist as portrayed...in newspaper cartoons;"* Joe Mott's face is *"mildly negroid in type;"* Piet Wetjoen is *"A Dutch farmer type."* Where the word is not mentioned, the idea remains; James Cameron has *"a quality about him of a prim, Victorian old maid."* Cecil Lewis *"is as obviously English as Yorkshire pudding and just as obviously the former army officer."* McGloin has *"the occupation of policeman stamped all over him."* Ed Mosher *"looks like an enlarged, elderly, bald edition of the village fat boy."* While the typicality of Willie Oban and of the bartender Rocky is not stressed (although Rocky is summarized as a *"Neapolitan-American"*), they are not essentially different from the other members of the chorus. The same is true of the three women: Pearl and Margie are called *"typical dollar streetwalkers,"* and Chuck Morello, the daytime bartender, like his night-time counterpart, is seen as an *"Italian-American."* Harry Hope, the chorus leader, is not viewed as typical in the same way. He maintains a certain individuality partly because it is through him that the liaison is made between the actions of the chorus and the principals. These—Larry Slade, Don Parritt and Theodore Hickman—are individuals, less by their appearance than by the complexity of their emotional problems.

The tableau thus formed, although externally static, has a powerful inner movement. The unity of the chorus is achieved by a remarkable theatrical tour de force. Each of the derelicts has, in the Stanislavskian sense, the same essential action: to foster himself in his dream. The actions create the unity of the microcosm O'Neill has woven. Against its fabric, the protagonists stand sharply drawn. Parritt, Slade and Hickey are seen, perhaps, as aspects of the same man. They overlap at least, in their acts of betrayal, their despairing desire to be rid of pity, their refusal to enter the world of the dreaming chorus. Yet, although they resemble one another, they stand opposed as antagonists as well, forming a hostile triangle against the unity of the background.

The physical picture awakens echoes of other works. O'Neill has evidently had his eye on Gorky's *The Lower Depths,* a play which he appreciated as "the great proletarian revolutionary play," saying that "it is really more wonderful propaganda for the submerged than any other play ever written, simply because it contains no propaganda, but simply shows humanity as it is—truth in terms of human life." The relation between the two works bears analysis as does the relationship between O'Neill's play and Ibsen's *The Wild Duck,* which like *The Iceman Cometh* explores the fatal effects of the "life-lie." In configuration and dramatis personae, Harry Hope's birthday party bears a strong resemblance to the traditional images of "The Last Supper." Such parallels are just and important and in part serve to explain why *The Iceman Cometh* now ranks among the most ambiguous of O'Neill's plays and has received the most extensive critical attention. In its original production, which marked the end of O'Neill's absence from the theatre, and in its 1956 revival in New York, a production that began the resurgence of interest in O'Neill's dramas, it has held a special position in the canon.

Yet viewed in its place in the progress of O'Neill's playwriting career it is not an ambiguous work. In part, it stands as an ironic comment on much that had preceded. Reverting to his earlier manner, spinning an all-but-plotless play filled with portraits of the down-and-out characters he had known as a young man, he recapitulates many of his early themes, particularly that of the "hopeless hope," but removes the romantic coloration with which he clothed the concept in *The Straw,* seeing it now, as he was to show it again in *Hughie,* as the only lifeline man could find.

The title, drawn from the story of the wise and foolish virgins in Matthew 25:6, parodies the description of the coming of the Savior: "But at midnight there was a cry made, 'Behold the bridegroom cometh.'" The savior who comes to Harry Hope's saloon is a strange messiah. The image of the iceman, suggestive of the chill of the morgue, and of a variety of off-color stories and songs featuring the iceman as a casual seducer, is interpreted by Willie Oban as meaning death: "Would that Hickey or Death would come." Hickey is a messiah of death, but his message, judged by its effect on its hearers, is closely parallel to that of O'Neill's other messiah, Lazarus of Bethany.

O'Neill's two choric dramas, both with titles derived from the New Testament, are at once remarkably alike and startlingly different from one another. In both *The Iceman Cometh* and *Lazarus Laughed*, a messianic figure appears preaching salvation to a world represented in microcosm by type characters. In each play, the recipients of the message prove resistant to it, and when it is forced upon them, prove incapable of acting in accord with it. In each, the messiah is set free to follow his own path to martyrdom by the murder of his wife. That path leads to burning—at the stake and in the electric chair. Such parallels are meaningless except as they relate to the central matter: the messages both messiahs preach, however different in effect and intention, are in essence the same. In a note for *Lazarus Laughed* O'Neill wrote "Death is the Father, Fear the Holy Spirit, Pain the Son." To this trinity man pays his homage. Lazarus's message to rid men of fear and pain is that they should see life as illusory, give over the dreams that haunt them like ghosts in the dark and acknowledge with clear eyes that they are part of life itself and can ask no higher good. Only then will they know the peace they instinctively seek. Lazarus's doctrine is a lonely one; he loves humanity but has little room for tenderness and for individual love. Miriam must follow unnoticed behind him, yearning for the simplicity of her life in the hills of Bethany. Those who accept his paradox, that death is life, lose human contact and the powers of sympathy, hope, humility and belief in man. Caught in the Dionysian ecstasy of his laughter, they throw themselves on the swords of soldiers. It is a chill rendition of Matthew, 10:39: "He who loses his life for my sake will find it."

Hickey's remedy for the ills of the world, as that world is represented by the types in Harry Hope's back room, is equally cold, equally predicated on a belief that human life is an illusion. As Lazarus exhorts, so Hickey, by means of a series of long, brutal individual encounters in the rooms above the bar, forces the dreamers to give over their ultimate link with life, the sustaining pipe dream of their worth as human beings. Their dreams hold at least an illusion of life's essence: movement in purposive action. Action, to be sure, will never be taken, but the dreams reveal a basic human truth: to foster life, man must preserve a minimal dream of movement. Hickey, whose promised peace is predicated on showing the dreamers that they will never take action and that their dream of doing so is a lie, brings the peace of death. Like much psychiatric theory, Hickey's Godless theology seeks "adjustment" to a meaningless reality, claiming that he who faces his life will find it. Yet if there is no life to be found, Hickey—not unlike Lazarus—becomes Death's priest.

The world which the dreamers inhabit has the fragile ecology of a tide pool. O'Neill calls the saloon "The Bottom of the Sea Rathskeller," and the imagery of drifting tidal life is pervasive. It is a world that barely holds to the fringes of consciousness, moving hesitantly between sleeping and waking, fusing the two conditions into a continuous trance-like existence. The light that filters through the dirty windows from the street is pale and insufficient to separate day from night. Time is meaningless. Voices are nearly unheard in the comatose silence. Existence at Harry Hope's is reduced to its lowest denominator, a hibernation of animals huddled together in dread of waking.

The dreamers have come to Hope's because, ostensibly, they are failures in the outside world, but their typicality makes it impossible to read their communal condition in terms of individual weakness. What lies outside is a world without value, a hostile society to which no man can possibly belong, and from which they must take refuge. At one point, Hickey mocks one of the men, saying, "You can't hang around all day looking as if you were scared the street outside would bite you!" But the menace in the streets is real. The threatening automobile that Harry Hope conjures up to justify his failure to take the walk around the neighborhood is, however imaginary, real. It is a symbol of a mechanized, spiritless world, a world in which God is dead.

After the long, poetically oriented quest which he had conducted through the plays of the 1920's, seeking a God to which men could belong, O'Neill at last has come to agree with Nietzsche that men live in a Godless world. There is no longer the possibility of being possessed by Dionysian ecstasy. Men's dreams can have no fulfillment that is not in itself illusion; the mindless, unpoetic materialism of each of the dreams is sufficient testimony to the fact that in all the outer world there is nowhere to go, nothing worth having, nothing to which man may make offering as to a God. In the wake of Hickey's teaching, men are left as walking corpses wandering in an icy hell; all they can do is to wait for death. In *Waiting for Godot*, Samuel Beckett describes the same interminable course of life, as Gogo and Didi indulge in senseless repetitious discourse and vaudeville routines to pass time. The pipe dreams of O'Neill's characters have the same function: they make life tolerable while the dreamers wait for Hickey or Death. As much as each of the dreamers permits himself to understand anything, he knows that the pipe dreams, his own included, are a game, that they are not real. Each man mocks the dreams of the others as insubstantial and illusory, but the mockery is a defensive irony, an essential element of the self-identification the individual's dreams provide. What cannot be admitted is pity, for pity would acknowledge the truth each seeks to conceal from himself. Nietzsche said God died of such pity; in self-pity the lowest creature will come to despair.

For the dreamers, a deliberately fostered illusion is the sign of membership in the club. The subject of the pipe-dream is unimportant. Some dreams, like Hugo Kalmar's incoherent anarchist ravings, are little more than fragmented, formless memories, holding so little sense of life as to be meaningless. But whether or not the dream is co-herent and contains a goal of action, its value lies less in its shape than that it forms part of the structure of illusion that "gives life to the whole misbegotten mad lot" of dreamers. The saving possibility is the mutu-ality of the dreamers' condition, for the conjunction of the dreams, the body heat of sleeping animals, provides the warmth of the world. This fact too makes it possible for the dreamers to hope without desire.

The world in which they live exists beyond desire. Whiskey alone sustains physical life. Hunger for food is not expressed, and no-tably no movement of sexual desire disturbs the quiet. The three whores arouse no one to lust, nor do they try to become objects of de-sire among the dreamers. Even the proposed marriage of Chuck and Cora is based on other dreams than that of sexual gratification. Very different from the Cycle plays, where sexual battles are fought to the death in an arena of passion, Hope's saloon is a world without women. Nevertheless, as in the Cycle plays, the power of woman is felt, and here, too, it is a destructive power.

Hickey's wife, Evelyn, is dead. Rosa Parritt, Don Parritt's moth-er and Larry Slade's former mistress, has gone to the death of spirit her imprisonment will bring upon her. Yet the power of these women, car-ried into the dreamers' world by the men who have loved them, de-stroys for a time the structure of life fostered there. In the Cycle plays, Deborah and Sara attempt to use Simon, to destroy his dreams and rid themselves of his desire. Rosa Parritt is pictured as an independent, fierce-willed woman who has held possessively onto her son at the same time as she has refused his love. His claim is that she has forced him into the radical movement, yet has permitted him no freedom of mature judgement. At the same time, he makes clear that he wants her to be his mother and resents her flaunting her lovers in the name of "Free Love." Her lover, Larry Slade, has left her in anger, calling her whore for much the same reason, so that a bond between Larry and Parritt exists that is like, if it is not in fact, that between father and son, and both feel guilty at having betrayed Rosa in order to be free of her rejection of their love. To love Rosa, a man must submit himself completely to her ambitions, but must make no demands in return. Betrayal is a defensive movement of their individuality.

On the other hand, Hickey's wife has made no ostensible demands on her husband. Hickey's description of her conveys the image of a gentle creature, the opposite of Rosa Parritt, but one who in a different way saps a man's individuality. She asks nothing, fears her husband's attention, yet her capacity for forgiveness, her confident faith in him proves to be as destructive as Rosa's independence. Like Margaret in The *Great God Brown,* Evelyn cannot see what is behind Hickey's face, even when he forces her brutally to look upon it. The blindness of her love makes Hickey live true to her dreams of him and fills him with guilt when he betrays her, just as Parritt and Slade are guilty in their compulsive betrayal of Rosa. O'Neill in the past, sensing that man must belong to some force that controls his being, had shown that those who ran from such possession were in the end caught and destroyed by it. In *The Iceman Cometh,* as in the Cycle plays, the force, devoid of its theological implications and reduced to a sexual relationship, has the same effect. Parritt has betrayed his mother to the police, Hickey has murdered Evelyn, and Larry must send his "son" to his death to end his torment, resigning himself finally to the sort of living punishment that Lavinia Mannon accepts in *Mourning Becomes Electra.* Each seeks death as the only way of assuaging or atoning for the guilt the woman has thrust upon him.

The three betrayers are the only occupants of the saloon who need pity. They epitomize, perhaps, the men without dreams who live in the hostile streets beyond the barroom door. They come, at least, from such a world, and disturb the dreaming sea. Both Hickey and Parritt force pity into the waters, but it is pity without tenderness. Parritt demands that Slade take pity on him and punish him by commanding him to suicide. Hickey, who insists that Larry's instinctive sympathy for the dreamers is the wrong kind of pity, attempts to rip off their masks and free them of the torture of hope. The play charts his failure and notes as well the way returning illusion brings life again to the sterile waters. When he has gone, old currents move again at the bottom of the sea, and the men who have been wakened to a hideous and intolerable truth begin to dream again.

The Iceman Cometh reflects the despair O'Neill himself felt in the year of its composition. On September 11, 1939, he wrote to Langner from Tao House:

The whole business from 1918 to now has been so criminally, hoggishly stupid. That is what sticks in one's gorge, that man can never learn but must be always the same old God damned greedy, murderous, suicidal ass! I foresee a world in which any lover of liberty will continue to live with reluctance and be relieved to die.

That it would be a relief to die! The desire that surges to the surface of the lives of the three betrayers in the play was a common reaction in that year. O'Neill was not alone.

The death of the human spirit remained his theme. Shortly, he set to work on a play entitled *The Last Conquest*: "The World-Dictator fantasy of a possible future, and the attempted last campaign of Evil to stamp out even the unconscious memory of Good in Man's spirit...." But the play remained in scenario, and *The Iceman Cometh* was withheld from production because, as he told Langner, "A New York audience could neither see nor hear its meaning. The pity and tragedy of defensive pipe dreams would be deemed downright unpatriotic...but after the war is over, I am afraid...that American audiences will understand a lot of *The Iceman Cometh* only too well."

Yet, as O'Neill had shown, the fostering of illusion bred a certain comfort that was a protection from despair. As a kind of epilogue to *The Iceman Cometh*, the following year, he attempted to make what was positive there more explicit, to write with a charity that was beyond pity and more like love of those whose souls stir in shadows. The play was *Hughie*, the first of six contemplated one-act plays to be given the group title, *By Way of Obit*. Of the six only one other was written more fully than an outline. This play, possibly concerning an old Irish chambermaid, was destroyed, together with the outlines and scenarios when the O'Neills left Tao House. But *Hughie* was left to reiterate with a difference the themes of *The Iceman Cometh*.

The fifty-minute play is an epitome of O'Neill's mature theatrical style and statement. A circle of light in a surrounding outer darkness that serves as a refuge in a hostile world whose presence is indicated by a consistent pattern of sounds; the passage of time so meaningless as to suggest an action outside of time; dialogue that is in essence two parallel almost uninterrupted monologues; characters who wear masks to conceal the agony of their inner lives; the image of life on the bottom of a sordid world where men's dreams provide the only warmth: what began so abortively in *A Wife for a Life* is here wrought into a perfect dramatic poem. The lyric mode of the play is abetted by the absence of any significant narrative plotting. The play depends on a purely emotional action evolved from the relationship established between Erie and Hughes, the Night Clerk. The dialogue, expressed in the rhythms and slang of Broadway argot of 1928, is used with the same awareness of its beauty and emotional power that Synge found in the dialect of the peasants of the Aran Islands. Like *The Iceman Cometh* and *A Moon for the Misbegotten* the action hinges on a tale to be told. Yet when it is set out, Erie's tale is no more than the vague account of lost affection, another expression of need, a lyric within a lyric.

The emotional center of the play perhaps evolves less from its words than from its silence. Such sounds as are heard in the hotel lobby—garbage cans, an El train, a fire engine and the like—accentuate the macabre stillness of a city in the early morning hours. The silence is a threatening force, an abnormal *"spell"* that *"presses suffocatingly upon the street, enters the deserted, dirty lobby."* To the Clerk, the night seems like death, and his mind *"cowers"* from it. Such hope as there is exists in the sounds that are the night's *"obsequies:"* *"Only so many El trains pass in one night, and each one passing leaves one less to pass, so the night recedes, too, until at last it must die and join all the other long nights in Nirvana, the Big Night of Nights. And that's life."* In the acted play, the Clerk's silence is to Erie like the silence of the city. The actor who plays Hughes must play but not speak the interior monologue. Only a few words rise to the surface; to Erie, he must seem another manifestation of death, like the threat outside, like Room 492 to which he cannot bear to return. Yet Hughes's silence is turning with a little life, born of vague hostilities, of physical pain in his feet, of boredom with overfriendly, anonymous hotel guests. Draped over the desk, he resembles a wax-works figure, but his mind pursues the sound he hears in destructive fantasies of waking *"the whole damned city"* with the garbage cans or of burning it down. It is only when an abnormally long pause of silence falls that he is forced out from the fantasies to hear the night sound nearest him, the voice of Erie Smith: *"His mind has been trying to fasten itself to some noise in the night, but a rare and threatening pause of silence has fallen on the city, and here he is, chained behind a hotel desk forever, awake when everyone else in the world is asleep, except Room 492, and he won't go to bed, he's still talking, and there is no escape."*

Erie pours words into the silence, words that spatter and drain away unheard. They are a bragging, wise-cracking lament that centers on his loss of his dead friend, the former Night Clerk, Hughie, with whom he has played a nightly game of dice, ensuring that the clerk would suffer no loss. In the streets there lies a physical threat of a beating from the men from whom he borrowed money to buy flowers for Hughie's funeral, and whom he cannot pay back. But the real threat is not physical: "I wouldn't never worry about owing guys, like I owe them guys. I'd always know I'd make a win that'd fix it. But now I got a lousy hunch when I lost Hughie I lost my luck—I mean, I've lost the old confidence. He used to give me confidence."

For "confidence," read "life." Without Hughie, Erie falls in a void that is like death. He cannot bring himself to enter the cage of the elevator and ascend to Room 492. Instead he stands twirling his room key, *"frantically as if it were a fetish which might set him free."* To leave the light of the lobby, to go through the door for which he has the key is to die. Erie clings to the key as if it were the substance of his life, as if life itself were somehow a key to death. Buying the hundred-dollar floral piece for Hughie's funeral to give him a *"big-time send-off"* has been the fulfilling act of his life. Accepting this, he also accepts that life holds nothing more for him, that he would be better off like Hughie, out of the racket his life has been. His mask has worn thin, and the darkness beneath shows through. At this point, he turns, defeated, and prepares to ascend to his room.

Yet his words have made contact, and in the play's final moments, the Night Clerk accepts the rules of Erie's fake dice game as Hughie had done. To Erie, the moment of realization that in the night he has touched another life is a *"saving revelation;"* to Hughes it is even more: *"Beatific vision swoons on the empty pools of the Night Clerk's eyes. He resembles a holy saint, recently elected to Paradise."* The vision of beatitude, a saint's vision, is no more than a pipe dream, but it is enough. What is perhaps unclear in *The Iceman Cometh* is explicit here, that man's only sense of life comes though sharing a vision with another human being. The vision has no truth; it contains no hope. Yet it offers movement, and it is the focus of existence. It is a far remove from the dreams of Robert Mayo or of Juan Ponce de Leon in *The Fountain,* who saw, or sought to see, God in their visions. No such matter animates Erie and the Night Clerk or those living in Harry Hope's back room. The pipe dream is only the way to sustain life; yet to dream is to endure.

The complex social imagery and the full psychological elaboration of the Cycle held O'Neill's interest through the beginning of 1939.

In that year, all solitudes were invaded, all walls broken. By June, the Cycle was unofficially shelved, and O'Neill had turned to writing about the lives of the down-and-outs in *The Iceman Cometh* and *Hughie,* as if, by retreating into the debris of humanity, he might find shelter from names like Munich, Czechoslovakia and Poland. The dreams that in the Cycle led a man toward action, out and into open warfare with his world, now changed, lost their power and became a form of memory as men turned weakly toward past illusions and huddled from the world. In bomb shelters, men do not behave very differently, perhaps, from the way they behave in *The Iceman Cometh.*

Dreams of Joy, Dreams of Pain

I found a rock the sea had washed over until it was shaped like a small, crowned head. The nose forms a strong, classic profile, and a hole cores through from side to side where eye-sockets should be. The mouth is a gash, curving like the letter "S," up one cheek and down the other. Viewed in profile from the right, it forms a perfect mask of tragedy, empty-eyed, the mouth pulled down in a distortion of pain. From the left, the face becomes the comic mask, the upward cut of the mouth fixing the stone in laughter.

The stone, of course, is not a work of art, except by so much as found objects may be admitted to a gallery. Its essential reality is that it is a piece of rock of a curious shape. Yet, depending on how that shape is viewed, it can also be taken as a curious symbol, now of tragedy, now of comedy and of the inter-relationship between the two.

Long Day's Journey into Night and *Ah, Wilderness!* are like the rock, once O'Neill's artistry is substituted for the tossing and erosion of water and wind and sand. O'Neill took a reality—certain events of his younger years—and formed them into two different structures of relationships, one comic, one tragic. It is not accurate to assume, as some have done, that *Ah, Wilderness!* is a comic treatment of the reality that *Long Day's Journey into Night* faithfully depicts. Both plays stem from reality, but neither presents it faithfully. Art never holds the mirror up to nature. It edits, distorts, shapes so that the artist's sense of what the experience meant or could have meant can be discerned.

Poets lie, as Plato said, and it is well for us that they do. To accept a lie is to spare ourselves much useless inquiry, such as wondering

Program note for the Milwaukee Repertory Company production of Long Day's Journey into Night *and* Ah, Wilderness! *in 1977.*

what Hamlet ate for breakfast. The erratic continuity of daily life is formless, even at its most memorable. What we remember of the times in our lives when we knew great joy or sorrow is as removed from the reality as a work of art is. In remembering, we edit, shape, find significance, and we eliminate the trivial and the tedious in ways we could never have done as we lived through the experience. Memory, like a poet, lies so that we may focus on what mattered.

So O'Neill, turning back compulsively to a period that was crucial in his memory, to a painful reality that shaped his art and his life, looked at the experiences and at members of his family and friends from a distance of space and time, and shaped his memories in order to rediscover the joys that existed in his New London boyhood, and once again to explore and understand the pain that darkened his life.

In the Preface to *A Dream Play,* August Strindberg, the Swedish dramatist to whom O'Neill was deeply indebted, speaks of writing a play that is like a dream:

> Characters divide, double, redouble, evaporate, condense, float out of each other, converge. But there is a consciousness transcending all—the consciousness of the dreamer. To it there are no secrets, no inconsistencies, no scruples, and there is no law. It neither judges nor absolves; it only relates. And since the dream usually contains more pain than pleasure, a tone of melancholy and compassion runs through the shifting narrative. The part that sleep, the liberator, plays is often painful; but when the pain seems at its worst, the sufferer wakes up to be reconciled to reality, which, however tormenting it may be, is still at that moment—and in contrast to the dream—a joy.

The passage is curiously pertinent to O'Neill's writing of *Long Day's Journey into Night,* and it is relevant that O'Neill claimed to have dreamed the whole of *Ah, Wilderness!* so that its writing was simply a matter of recording his dream. Artistically, O'Neill was entirely in sympathy with Strindberg, whom he once praised for doing more than hold the family Kodak up to ill-nature. Like many of Strindberg's works, O'Neill's comedy and tragedy are "dream plays," pervaded by the shaping awareness of the dreamer-playwright, through whose vision the audience is empowered to see into the past.

On its surface, *Long Day's Journey into Night* may seem "real" enough, but examine the controls that shape the events of a day into a symbolic journey that is like a life-time. Most apparently, there is the weather, a bright day that turns gray and darkens as the fog rolls in, until the world is blotted out and the family is hidden in the night. They must live in their cage-like room for what seems an eternity. At the end nothing exists outside that room except darkness and cold and the meaningless bleat of the foghorn crying in a void.

The scene, at first, is full of the furnishings of ordinary lives: clothes, furniture, books, food. But as the play progresses, these things are forgotten and lost in shadow. The scene diminishes until all that can be touched are a table, a bottle, a playing card, a light bulb. The house becomes no more than a small circle of light in illimitable darkness, and in this circle, finally, the Tyrones explore themselves and their inter-relationships.

Such a dispensing of externals is always an element in great tragedy. Oedipus, his pride destroyed, becomes in Yeats's phrase "a paltry thing... A tattered cloak upon a stick." King Lear, in the midst of the storm on the heath, tears at his clothes so that, naked, he may better understand "unaccommodated man." The Tyrones, set adrift in the fog, come to the essentials of what they are and discover the sole accommodating thing that will give their lives substance.

The hush that descends in the last moments of the play brings the anodyne of silence all have sought. In dope, in drinks, in dreams, the four have groped toward a center where they can drift as in a noiseless sea. Longing for such a state of forgetfulness, Edmund, Eugene's persona in the play, says "I would have been much more successful as a seagull or a fish." Like him, the others seek for similar surcease from the pain of loss in their lives.

What causes their agony is the memory of promise. Edmund, sensing the need they all have to hold to what has gone by, speaks of certain memories as being like "a saint's vision of beatitude," meaning by the phrase his own need to lose his individuating consciousness and to enter into nature, as water flows into water. Mary's beatitude is the memory of her girlhood faith and her music. James's is the artist's command he once possessed, to which Edwin Booth, America's finest actor, paid tribute. No such memory exists for Edmund's brother, who can only howl for blessing like a soul in hell.

Why have they become like this? Why can they not change? In "reality" they did. Eugene recovered from his tuberculosis and became America's greatest dramatist. He and his father were reconciled and became respectful friends. His mother, with the help of the sisters of her church overcame her addiction to morphine and after her husband's death took control of her life and Jamie's. As she recovered, Jamie gave over drinking while she lived. In short, in the reality, there was hope, but O'Neill edited it out. It was not part of the dream of pain.

In the dream, we repeatedly hear that "God is dead." Edmund quotes the phrase from Nietzsche, whose works his father finds poisonous. Yet, in the existential, fog-bound world, God indeed seems dead. Edmund's desire to move behind the veil of nature is only a desire to lose awareness of himself. Mary's faith is a memory of lost illusion. Like the others, they must exist in a world that cannot offer a hope of such a hereafter as will give order and meaning to their lives on earth.

The greatest tragedy is always God-guided. A divinity shapes the end, and man is measured by his power to understand himself in relation to that end. His guilt must be acknowledged, his responsibility asserted, his atonement made. This accomplished, he can claim both triumph and the right to peace.

Yet when God is dead, what final atonement can be made? When guilt is pervasive and responsibility meaningless, how can man triumph or find peace? As O'Neill narrows and deepens his image of the Tyrones, he causes them to pass beyond the personal and the particular and become nearly universal images of persons caught in an existential dilemma. He will have none of the tragi-comic despair of Beckett's dramas or of the acid philosophical depictions of the plays of Sartre or Camus. He seeks another value. The lonely blind can find no comfort except in dreaming and in sharing dreams so they can touch other dreamers. In the end, these souls talk of their loss and of their need, and they reach out to find vestiges of sympathy and love. It is a far cry from the heroic conclusion of earlier tragedies that spoke of such assurance as love and the courage to endure and the power of life to continue even in darkness. Yet O'Neill's play is made of the same subject matter, and asserts as did Shakespeare and the Greek dramatists the need for human beings to find a way to come to terms with their humanity.

By contrast *Ah, Wilderness!* seems a very different play, a nostalgic portrait of a turn-of-the-century, small American town on the Fourth of July. Like the tragedy, it too follows a day from early morning to late at night, but the world it depicts is never effaced. It is full of things—firecrackers, furniture, lobsters, music—and it is joyful and promises benison to young and old.

It is a remarkably protected world. In this it is like the Forest of Arden in *As You Like It* or the woods in *A Midsummer Night's Dream*. Nothing bad is allowed to happen within its confines. No one really gets hurt (Aunt Lily perhaps excepted), but instead the action offers love fulfilled and the continuity of life maintained. This, of course, is the unchanging theme of non-satiric comedy: Life will continue; men and women will live in harmony with nature, and because they do, will find happiness. The end of such comedy is the ceremony of the wedding, a rite that sanctifies the course of the wooing.

O'Neill, to be sure, only points to the wedding, but the final lines in the play, spoken as Nat and Essie watch their son, Richard, moving into the moonlight "like Love's Young Dream," testify to the rightness of life's cycle, a joyful day's journey to fulfillment.

That the natural cycle is right is the lesson the persons of the comedy must learn. Here, as in *Twelfth Night* the characters struggle to pull away from what is right, that which is in accordance with nature's cycle. Richard does his best to follow his literary masters, Ernest Dowson, Henrik Ibsen, Oscar Wilde, into a stranger, darker world, but he is not allowed to do so. Nature has cast a spell on him, and protects him, much as Oberon protects the lovers in the midsummer woods, using his magic to bring them to harmony.

To consider how O'Neill transforms the reality of his life to this comic vision is instructive as to the process of the artist's "editing." It would have been simple to have eliminated all the negatives that are brought to the fore in *Long Day's Journey into Night,* but the result, probably, would have been a work of saccharine sentiment. The negatives belong here, and O'Neill does not overlook them—the failed responsibility, the personal dereliction—nor does he turn his back on pain. Yet he finds a way to present these things so that the family's life is not destroyed.

Strindberg's comment that in a dream play characters divide and double is helpful. It is not his brother who tempts Richard to visit the tavern, but rather the brother's friend. The woman he meets there is not a brothel whore, but a "swift baby" from New Haven. It is not the mother who fails her maternal obligations and turns to a kind of girlish spinsterhood as she rejects her family. That role is given to Aunt Lily, just as James Tyrone's drinking and tavern-rounding are left for jovial Uncle Sid. Both Lily and Sid are American comic stereotypes, the old maid and the amiable drunk. As with all stereotypes, we are shown little of them and so their capacity to cause pain is diminished, Yet their presence permits O'Neill to suggest the negatives at the same time as he relieves the father and the mother of serious failings. In the end, the questions of guilt and failed responsibility are not raised in such a way as to hurt us or haunt us.

The reality, O'Neill's life as it was actually lived in New London, lies at the source of both plays. O'Neill moves pain aside in the comedy, but he knows that joy and pain are intermingled and shift as light shifts. *Long Day's Journey into Night,* after all, begins in laughter and light, with only occasional hints of what is to come.

It is odd that *Ah, Wilderness!* came to O'Neill in a dream. Perhaps his mind was casting back over the reality, seeking some way to alter the truth so as to make it bearable, to edit out the pain that, when he awoke, continued to haunt him. Dreams are expressive of need and for O'Neill, as the Tao House plays make clear, the need was to make all right, to atone, and to find a way to forgive and be forgiven. In *Long Day's Journey into Night* and its sequel about his brother, *A Moon for the Misbegotten,* the playwright tried valiantly to face the essence of his life by recreating the structure of his family's relationships. The attempt meant he had to endure again the pain of the reality as it was held in memory. Such an attempt is a form of atonement, even though the forgiveness has only the ephemeral and symbolic shape of a dream.

About *A Touch of the Poet*

A *Touch of the Poet* is a magnificent relic, the only finished play of Eugene O'Neill's greatly conceived Cycle of plays on American historical subjects. Had he been able to complete the eleven plays in his plan, the Cycle could only have been compared with Shakespeare's two cycles on British history.

The Cycle, whose theme O'Neill announced in his title, "A Tale of Possessors Self-Dispossessed," centered on the lives of a New England family, the Harfords, and traced the careers of various members from the years before the Revolutionary War to the 1930's. Against the background of major events of American history, O'Neill told of the men and women of this country who had once been offered an opportunity to live in peace, in the bounty of nature. Their greed, however, destroyed all that lay before them and turned their vision to idle dreams. Ironically, they refused to deny their dreams and were therefore condemned to lives of frustrated, empty hope.

A Touch of the Poet, which O'Neill completed on November 13, 1942, was the fifth play of what had begun in 1934 as a cycle of seven plays, but which expanded to eleven as O'Neill developed his theme and his characters. It was hammered through in spite of protracted illness, including a tremor that at times made writing impossible. Still, as one of the Tao House plays it is a major work of his finest period of playwriting, written in the same years as *Long Day's Journey into Night, The Iceman Cometh, Hughie,* and *A Moon for the Misbegotten.*

Although it is different in tone and apparent subject matter from the great autobiographical plays, *A Touch of the Poet* has much in

Program note for a production of A Touch of the Poet *at The Longwharf Theatre, New Haven, CT, 1992.*

common with the companion works, particularly *The Iceman Cometh*, whose characters, like Cornelius Melody, the central figure of the historical play, can only survive in the world of their dreams.

Melody, a once proud Irish soldier, who claims to have owned a castle in Ireland, has fought with Wellington in Spain, but an amatory escapade has led to his disgrace. He has come to America and purchased a down-at-the-heels tavern on a little used post-road near Boston. There, he manages a meager living with his wife, Nora, and their daughter, Sara. The only vestiges left to him of his former pride are his old uniform and the memories it brings, and a fine mare that is an emblem of the life he has lost. The relics form a mask he wears to hide the emptiness within him.

Nora, an unabashed peasant woman, loves him without criticism, but Sara finds his Byronic posing distasteful and lashes him with unmerciful contempt. As the play develops, her love for the son of the rich Harford family leads to Melody's "unmasking" by a savage beating from the Harford servants. Giving over all pretense, he shoots the mare and in so doing destroys his mask of pride. He reverts to the character of an Irish bog-trotting peasant at the play's end.

In his story, O'Neill points to the necessity of dreams to sustain life, but he also shows the destructive power of a dream that has no valid reality. Dreams save, but they also destroy—a bitter maxim O'Neill found applicable to the American dream itself.

In the plays that were to follow *A Touch of the Poet*, O'Neill planned to trace the failure of the dream in the lives of the sons of Sara and her husband, Simon Harford. The next play, *More Stately Mansions*, tells of Simon's change from a dreaming philosopher like Henry David Thoreau to a powerful manipulator of men and money, and of the fate of his mother, Deborah, who seeks to escape life by succumbing to a dream that is in itself madness. *More Stately Mansions*, one of O'Neill's most disturbing plays, exists in an unrevised draft that has been performed in drastically cut form in New York, Los Angeles and Stockholm.

The sequent plays of the Cycle were destroyed, but surviving scenarios and notes show that they were to trace the lives of the sons of Sara and Simon on a clipper ship sailing around the Horn, in San Francisco in the 1840's, and thereafter at various locations around the world—New York, Washington, Paris, Japan and finally, in the 1930's, Detroit, where Sara's great-granddaughter was to become a power in the automobile industry. Remaining central to the story is the aging, indomitable Sara who rules the Melody-Harford clan. Her use of her power brings to focus a major sub-theme concerning the destruction of men by the women they worship.

As he began his final re-working of *A Touch of the Poet*, O'Neill noted in his work diary, "think may rewrite this to get at least one play of the Cycle definitely and finally finished." His concern that the Cycle would not be finished proved true. His illness led to a day in a Boston hotel when he faced the necessity of burning the incomplete or unrevised drafts. That day can be remembered as one of major loss to the world's theatre. Carlotta O'Neill said it was like burning one's children. In the one completed play there is an ample taste of what the quality of the whole would have been. The bravura roles are an exacting temptation to actors, and the thematic content a challenge to serious audiences. What O'Neill felt as his increasing incapacity made it impossible to express the conceptions that lay within him, and forced him to final silence is difficult to imagine without feeling profound pity for a writer of genius imprisoned by his own body.

The Monastery and the Prison

Perhaps as a consequence of my sins and certainly of my editorial commitments, I read during his centennial year upward of 3000 of Eugene O'Neill's letters and his complete works three times. I remember feeling as I read that my sins must have been unusually heavy to require such penance.

Yet there was a fascination in the work as well. When I started each time with the trivial vaudeville sketch, *A Wife for a Life*, and remembered that at the end of his creative life there lay *A Moon for the Misbegotten* and that frightening and baffling work, *More Stately Mansions*, I traced with undiminished commitment the course of a life in art that was in its way as unique as Proust's, as prolific as Shaw's, as tortured as Strindberg's. Reading in the detailed way an editor must, I often found myself less interested in the play at hand than in the man who at a slow tempo comparable to that of my reading set the words on paper. Tracing what he had written word for word, I sometimes felt a strong degree of identification with the playwright, even, in aberrant moments after a long day's duty, coming to think that his words were my words. At other times, what I read did not seem to be literally what I knew they were, a playscript, but part of a life-long confession called from the center of his being. When that happened, I would pull away, saying I am his editor, not his priest and get a cup of coffee to dispel the delirium. Yet the phenomenon recurred so strongly and often that I have felt it not inappropriate to speak of it. My reaction suggests to me a mystery of his character—the compulsion to confess, to make all public, but at the same time to disappear into an inviolable private world.

To my mind, no more moving description of an artist caught up in the agony of composition exists than the description by Carlotta O'Neill of her husband's behavior during the time he was writing *Long*

Presented to the American Literature Association in Baltimore, Maryland, June 1993.

Day's Journey into Night: "When he started *Long Day's Journey,* it was a most strange experience to watch that man being tortured every day by his own writing. He would come out of his study at the end of a day gaunt and sometimes weeping. His eyes would be all red and he looked ten years older than when he went in in the morning...."

The creative stress was merciless, and sometimes, O'Neill seems to have moved in a semi-trance as the illusory imaginings and the real memories which formed his subject matter coalesced into a burden of sorrow and guilt demanding confession and the absolution only his art could provide. His houseman, Herbert Freeman, told me that sometimes as he emerged from his study O'Neill would pass him on the stairway without returning his greeting or seeming to see him. Later, realizing he had committed what might have appeared to be a discourtesy, O'Neill would apologize, saying that he was so lost in his writing he was sometimes unaware of what passed around him. It was as if in rising from sleep, his mind had held to the traceries of dream, so that he moved during the day in light and half light, aware, but also a little beyond diurnal consciousness.

Tao House, built on a small meadow against a California hillside, rests in bright sunshine. When O'Neill lived there, it was surrounded by walnut groves; orange trees that he planted still line the walks outside the house. Inside, however, it is shadowy. The thick concrete bricks of the walls keep out the changes of weather. The widely spaced windows admit daylight sparingly. Light reflected from dark mirrors creates a crepuscular atmosphere. Speaking of the gray mirror hung on a wall of his bedroom, O'Neill said that he loved it "because I look like a ghost."

It was not entirely a joke, as Mrs. O'Neill's description of the haunted man emerging from his study at the day's end suggests. To the study he went to suffer with his ghosts, to meditate and, finally, to write in painful struggle. The study is a small room, fourteen by seventeen feet. What is most interesting about it is its isolation. It is placed on the second floor at the extreme southern end of the house, far from any centers of domestic activity. It is cut off from the house by three doors, one to the room itself, one to O'Neill's wardrobe placed in a short corridor between his bedroom and the study, and finally, the bedroom door. With the three doors closed, no sound penetrates. Nothing is to be seen through two of the windows, and the view of Mount Diablo from the east window is a remote prospect, an unintrusive background with no articulated interest.

Tao House provided the ultimate isolation O'Neill needed in which to write, but he had always required similar isolated spaces. At Monte Cristo Cottage when he began his playwriting career, he worked on a second story sun-porch. At Peaked Hill Bar, on Cape Cod, he had the relative isolation of a second floor studio; in the château at Le Plessis, the study was in a "tourelle" on one of the building's corners; in Georgia, his study, again remotely placed, was arranged like the cabin of a ship with small, porthole-like windows that suggested he was writing miles from shore, surrounded by the limitless, undisturbing ocean.

All writers, no doubt, prefer quiet and isolation in which to work, but not all are in effect silenced when they cannot commandeer such space. Outwardly convivial, a genial, if quiet man, O'Neill was friendly and responsive in the ordinary intercourse of daily existence. He had firm friendships; people liked him well. But when he was at work his behavior changed. Then those about him were forced to endure his moody silences and the malaise which, as he grew older and his work sought out new tragic depths, increasingly surrounded his creative life. When the world forced its way in on him, as it did during his divorce from Agnes O'Neill, when his children, Shane and Oona, seemed to him to fall from reputable standards of conduct, and when the war in Europe broke out, his writing was affected seriously. When the work was not there to do, as on the ill-fated trip to the Orient, he lost control of himself and damaged his closest ties. Without the work he was lessened as a human being.

In *Long Day's Journey into Night*, the sons of James Tyrone mock their father for his lecture on "the value of a dollar" and the necessity of hard work. Nevertheless, O'Neill learned his father's lesson well, and throughout his active life, once he left the tuberculosis sanitarium and settled down to write, he worked constantly. Many another writer has worked as continually and as diligently as O'Neill; not many have been so work-obsessed. No doubt the unrelenting self-discipline resulted from the creative pressure within him. One senses in him always a race against time—to get *this* finished that *that* may progress. His productivity, taken together with the high artistry of his work, was astonishing. Work was life.

To carry out the work, he required special facilities, at least from the time of writing *Mourning Becomes Electra* forward. The account he kept in his work diary of the writing of the trilogy is a startling account of the days spent in the tourelle at Le Plessis. With scarcely any let-up he worked, re-worked and again re-worked the long text, adding masks and asides, throwing them out, cutting, expanding, restructuring and re-thinking the qualities of situation and character; then polishing almost continuously between 1929 and 1931 until the play was as it should be. Even then the work was not finished. As the play went into rehearsals, he cut and re-shaped it, working it over with the director, Philip Moeller, until it was fully ready for the stage. His total of "Working Days" recorded in his diary was 533, many of which he noted as "double days." The same sort of labor was to be required for *Days Without End* as he fought its stubborn undramatic shape through seven drafts—339 W.D.'s by his estimate. To come thereafter, beginning as early as 1928 with a play idea for a work to be titled "On to Betelgeuse," was a project that was to occupy him for the rest of his creative life, the Cycle, *A Tale of Possessors Self-dispossessed.*

The obsessive work in a silence as complete as he could arrange was only part of what was to emerge as a paradox of his creative life. In addition, there was his handwriting. He wrote with pen or pencil in a script that was far from normal. The plays are written in letters so tiny that they seem to be inscribed rather than penned. It has been said that such handwriting is characteristic of those with a tremor—that only by writing so tightly can they control the shaking of the hand. Yet in letters to friends, his hand is relatively normal in size and flowing cursiveness. Not so in his playscripts. All of *The Emperor Jones,* written in 1920 as he began his professional career, is written on three faces of two 8" x 11" sheets of paper. Corrections to the script of the uncompleted *More Stately Mansions* are written *between* the single spaced lines of the typed copy. The microscopic script almost seems like a riddling trick, a code to preserve the privacy of what he had written.

But what was at the heart of such writing? He found many ways of hiding it, but the core, as we now know, was an analysis of himself, his mother and father and importantly his brother, Jamie, whom he seems to have felt was his *doppelgänger,* the embodiment of the destructive part of himself, not easily assuaged. In a variety of fictional disguises, these four figures forced themselves upon him and became his constant concern. They stalked his imagination in memories of love and betrayal and hate. They were, as he called them, ghosts crying for exorcism. He fled from them, hiding in the privacy of his study, but there, by way of appeasing them, he conjured them in costumed images. It was not sufficient. They demanded to be acknowledged by more direct representation, by what amounted to confession and atonement.

During the years at Tao House, perhaps the life-time of privacy, the arduous loneliness, coupled with illness and the painfully difficult work on the Cycle became so unbearable that to open the doors to the imprisoning workhouse to the view of a curious world became the only anodyne. The room at Tao House may have seemed not so much a study as a cell, both a monastery and a prison, where he circled in through the long writing of the Cycle on the autobiographical plays that would finish and crown his work. Yet an important irony of his life is that the work accomplished in the most extreme isolation had to become a public statement, a confession. Only by sharing through his art the things he held most inviolate in his mind and heart could he silence the pursuing memories and bring peace to the ghosts in the gray mirror.

O'Neill's plays are walls of glass, and darkly through the glass, the man can always be glimpsed, stripped of the artist's persona, moving as a silent supernumerary on the stage he creates. Like Strindberg, O'Neill is a presence felt throughout his drama, the dreamer, the seeker, the sufferer.*

The past was not to be escaped. It emerged without his willing it. At his Georgia home, in September 1922, as he worked on the recalcitrant religious drama, *Days Without End*, a play that in retrospect can be seen to contain many autobiographical elements, a new idea came to him. In his diary, he recorded that he had worked on the religious play from midnight until 2:30 a.m. When he awoke the next morning, he had *Ah, Wilderness!* fully in mind, and by 9:00 a.m. he was at work on it. He wrote: "Awoke with idea for this 'Nostalgic Comedy' & worked out tentative outline—seems fully formed and ready to write." It was. He finished the first draft that same month, on September 22. By September 30, he began work with fresh insights on an old idea, "On to Betelgeuse," retitled "The Life of Bessie Bowen." From this work, the Cycle was to generate.

September, 1922, was creatively explosive. The first of the autobiographical plays and the Cycle both generated then. *Ah, Wilderness!*

---

* Such a ghostly presence accounts, perhaps, for the lyric thrust of the plays notably in the long, uninterrupted monologues that are often a threnody of longing and loss. A lyric is a poem to be sung, and the source of the song is the emotional inner life of the poet. It is ironic that those who have attempted to make operas of O'Neill's work have selected the heavily plotted plays, like *Mourning Becomes Electra* and *Ile* and ignored such lyrical pieces as *The Great God Brown* or *Lazarus Laughed*. In most of the major plays, there comes a time when a central character is given an aria-in-embryo and allowed to speak in solitude, out of silence. One thinks of many examples, such as Ephraim Cabot's account of his westward journey in *Desire Under the Elms* or Ezra Mannon's memory of the war in *Mourning Becomes Electra*. Sometimes it seems the characters speak less to one another or to the audience than to themselves. They are more overheard than heard. They are singers of melody-less songs, making lyrics of their inmost feelings, much the same as O'Neill appears to have done as he wrote in his solitude.

broke out of his mind, as it were, in a dream. Although it did not face the full truth of his early life but hid the truth under charming nostalgia, it marked the beginning of an almost uncontrollable movement toward the telling of his most personal truth. Defensively, his impulse was to stop almost at once, barring confession by turning to the newly conceived Cycle. However, the true story could not be repressed forever, and in the long, hard sessions at Tao House, the story of the Tyrones worked closer to the front of his mind.

As the years went along, in my reading of what went on in the study at Tao House, the tension created by his need to face his past grew. Perhaps the best evidence lies in the unfinished work, *More Stately Mansions,* the play designed to follow *A Touch of the Poet.* It is in four acts and an epilogue, eleven scenes in all. The only extant copy of the play is typed in about 500 single-spaced pages with O'Neill's corrections and emendations cramped between the lines. There are some indications of cutting. For example, the original Act IV, Scene 4 was cut in its entirety. Essentially, however, the play did not receive a final editing by O'Neill. In the first three acts he reworked passages and excised some repetitious encounters, but the dialogue in the fourth act has not been edited. The play remains a massive artifact whose true theatrical life will probably remain forever in doubt because of its great length. It does not have much stage action; its vitality lies in its talk. It would require between seven and eight hours—perhaps more—to perform.

The writing of the Cycle suggests a kind of madness in its author. From what has been learned of the plan for *A Tale of Possessors Self-dispossessed,* it seems doubtful that O'Neill would have finished the work, even had he been in the best of health in the best of all worlds. The tremor and other illnesses blocked him; the outbreak of war depressed him deeply, but even so, he managed to complete the autobiographical masterpieces which comprise the Tao House plays, but they were necessities bred of lifelong anguish. The Cycle can be looked on, as can many of his earlier plays, as a way of not writing the central truths of his life. Manuscripts seemed to grow of their own volition— 60,000 word drafts and scenarios which had to be divided into two plays so that the Cycle grew larger and larger. In the end, the Cycle was out of control and O'Neill had to destroy it.

Of the Cycle, he managed to put only *A Touch of the Poet* into acceptable theatrical form. On February 16, 1942, he noted in his Work Diary, "Cycle—A Touch of the Poet (5th in ll) (think I may rewrite this to get at least one play of the Cycle definitely & finally finished)." The remark perhaps has in it a tacit admission that the other plays will never be completed.

A Touch of the Poet stands somewhat outside the central story of the Harfords. Deborah Harford's recapitulation of the family history in Act II is an important link to the past and to the plays to come, but the play belongs to the new arrivals to the story, the Melodys, not the Harfords and so can stand more or less complete in itself. In writing *Mourning Becomes Electra,* he was concerned that each part of the trilogy should stand alone as a play at the same time as it carried forward the long narrative of the whole. The same problem concerned him in writing the Cycle. Each play should be a complete story despite the necessary interconnections to plays past and to come. Yet in the structure of the Cycle, *A Touch of the Poet* stands a little apart, just as the scene on Adam Brant's ship in *Mourning Becomes Electra* removes the action for a time from the Mannon house. It was, therefore, more readily to be completed than others which relied on fuller knowledge of the Harfords.

Through the fall of 1942, despite advancing illness, he restructured and rewrote *A Touch of the Poet* making it, finally, a thing complete in itself, relying on nothing beyond its own established conditions. *More Stately Mansions,* however, involved the entire Cycle. The major work on it was done between March, 1938 and January 20, 1939, when he noted in his diary that he had finished revising the third draft. In June, 1939, he wearily dropped the Cycle, writing in his Work Diary, "Decide what I've done on 5th play is n.g., so tear it up, Feel fed up and stale on Cycle after 4 1/2 years of not thinking of any other work—will do me good to lay on shelf and forget it for a while—do a play that has nothing to do with it." The next day he began to outline *The Iceman Cometh* and by the end of the month had started the outline for *Long Day's Journey into Night*. The confessional plays had at last thrust their way through. When he finished *The Iceman Cometh* at the end of the year, he turned briefly back to the Cycle and made notes for revisions. A month's illness when he wrote nothing followed. By February, 1940, he had again laid the Cycle aside to work on *Long Day's Journey into Night*. What he called "my interlude of war obsession" intervened, but by July, he wrote "am ready to go ahead with this play, deeply moved, am convinced I can make it one of my best." Perfunctory reworking of some of the Cycle plays, and several non-Cycle ideas occupied him after he had completed *Long Day's Journey into Night*, but it was not until the following October, 1941, that his creative energies returned at their full, and he started on *A Moon for the Misbegotten* which would involve, as he noted "Jamie's revelation of self." His work on *More Stately Mansions* and the other Cycle material appears to have been perfunctory, re-outlining and making notes for bringing the three sisters, the Norn-like rulers of the House of Harford, into the action.

Martha Bower, who has provided an authoritative edition of the play, states that *More Stately Mansions* is a finished work—this despite O'Neill's disclaimer on the title page of the typescript that it is "an unfinished work...to be destroyed in case of my death!" Bower claims, "The play is complete; the action is whole," but although the full story is told, the play is not "complete" in the sense that it is ready for the stage. O'Neill might have pruned it, but it is questionable that he was genuinely committed to shaping it for the theatre. His rewriting in the typescript seems listless. It does not suggest that he was ready to perform the needed radical surgery on what he had written, but rather that he was dealing with small matters of tone and attitude.

Cuts and slight changes of wording sharpen some of the dialogue, but they by no means reveal a professional playwright preparing his work for the theatre. Much of it is unstageable, and the dialogue might well stump the bravest actor. In the first scene of Act Three, for example, O'Neill causes his protagonist, Simon Harford, to meditate on his relationships with his wife, Sara, and his mother, Abigail,* recapitulating past action and vowing vengeance for the wrongs he feels the women to have done him. The monologue runs some 1600 words and there are no cuts indicated in it. Martha Bower compares it to Hickey's monologue at the end of *The Iceman Cometh*, which it rivals in length, but there is an important difference between the two. Hickey's monologue moves the play forward; it is an essential phase of the action. Simon's speech is static, advancing little, revealing nothing essential that has not been or will not be revealed in action. Arthur Miller comments that when O'Neill "indulged" in the long monologue, "his storytelling never stopped, and if it did, he failed." In Simon's monologue, despite its reminiscences, story-telling is overwhelmed by a somewhat superficial self-analysis and by an explicit, rather than dramatic commentary on Sara and Abigail. For example:

[Sara] is too preoccupied being the children's mother to have any love to spare—that, also, is part of Mother's scheme to dispossess me—(*irritably*) Rot! Forget your idiotic suspicions of her! That silly old woman's senile mind is too occupied with pretending contentment as a doting grandmother to engage in such elaborate conspiracy—although she is undoubtedly responsible for much of the indifference—but to return to Sara, hadn't I better think out more exactly how I shall attack?

"But to return to Sara..." Such academic prose has little to do with the character or, for that matter, with the theatre.

---

*In a late revision of *A Touch of the Poet*, O'Neill changed Abigail's name to Deborah.

Writing in so awkward and explicit a fashion, O'Neill appears to be thinking his way through the intricacies of his characters, exploring to find out what his people are, but caring little in the dramatist's sense for what they do. At times, there seems to be confusion between character and dramatist, as if O'Neill through the long character analysis were writing about himself rather than about his characters. Harford says:

> No, you must allow for your present state of mind—the reaction of emptiness after success—you've always felt it—But never so strongly before—there is a finality in this—as if some long patient tension had snapped—as if I'd reached the end of a blind alley in my mind where I no longer have the power to discipline my will to keep myself united—another self rebels—secedes—as if at last I must become two selves from now on—division and confusion—a war—a duel to the death.

O'Neill here might well be talking to and of himself.* Speaking of his illness, he once wrote to Eugene Jr., "When you live through the play you write, you have to have a lot of reserve life on tap," and Carlotta described evenings when her husband talked all night; "I shut up and didn't say a word." Some compulsion, almost uncontrollable, seemed to animate him. Speaking of the length of the drafts of the cycle, he wrote "they get that way in spite of me and my plans for them, and I don't want them to." Something, clearly, was wrong.

Throughout the manuscript, O'Neill evidences concern with the stage directions that indicate the tone of the speeches. To alter a stage direction is not to cut. O'Neill has spent more time on these revisions than on other aspects of the editing. The darkness of the play can be felt by merely listing some of these: *gloatingly, resentfully, contemp-*

---

* In her introduction to her edition of the play, Martha Bauer notes that the long monologue appears revelatory of O'Neill's most painful experience (p.9), and later she speaks of the "confessional material buried in the almost impenetrable writing."

tuously, irritably, with a little shudder, uneasily, regretfully, forcing a casual tone, with bitter hostility. These are taken more or less in order from the third scene in Act III, one in which the three principals, Simon Harford, his wife, Sara, and mother Abigail, sit in physical silence and speak their thoughts in what is to be understood as silent communion with one another. One word that continually recurs in the stage directions is *strangely*. It requires the actor to be suspicious, hostile, defensive, uneasy and mysterious, and though it is not quite definable, it is the term that governs the life of these people and the play in which they appear.

The scene is one of the most odd that O'Neill ever wrote. Mother, son and wife sit placidly, the women sewing, the man reading in what O'Neill calls a *"tense, eavesdropping silence."* They do not speak to one another, but commune by means of their ostensibly unspoken thoughts which are, O'Neill says, *"the meaning of the silence."* Beneath the surface the tension stretches taut to the breaking point as relationships are considered, discarded, reformed on new grounds. As their loathing for one another grows, O'Neill creates a miasma of hatred that wells like a thick mist over the stage. Simon's thoughts move in parallel to those of the women as he plots his campaign against their dominance. The women come into league against him with no outer word being spoken, until at the act's climactic moment the two women speak aloud one another's name and Sara moves to sit beside Abigail, forming an alliance against Simon. It is an extraordinary dramatic sequence, sure in its effect and right in its slow tempo.

For all such moments of brilliance, the question remains: what was O'Neill doing, there in that study, day in and day out, writing so compulsively of these gloating, greedy, hostile figures? Clearly when he began, he was concerned with the American as a waster of his inheritance, but these characters are not that. Greedy manipulators they are indeed—founders of the tribe of Robber Barons soon to follow them in the history that was to be delineated on his stage. Yet early on, the Cycle takes an inward turn that by the time of the writing of *More Stately*

Mansions has become something very different from a lament for the nation. The twisted psychological stories, telling of the greedy desires of the Harfords, override any commentary on the history of the United States. The Harfords as seen in the surviving notes for the later plays become monsters. No character (and *More Stately Mansions* is a case in point) engages the sympathies of an audience. The way O'Neill has them speak is the way they are: resentful, contemptuous, bitter, gloating, hostile. And unbearable.

How could he go day after day to write of these figures of an imagination that may well have needed an ounce of civet from some good apothecary? One almost has a sense that as he sat in his study writing long scenarios, detailed notes, and draft upon draft of the Harford saga that he was telling himself stories in order to preserve the illusion of normal working conditions. But always, the stories took an inner turn. Often in a scene what begins as normal dialogue will shift midway to become an inner monologue, sometimes intended to be heard, sometimes not. There is a recessive movement in the action and dialogue, a movement which comes to a head when Abigail steps into her summerhouse deliberately to seek out madness and to find the surcease she has hitherto sought in her garden where the sounds in the street beyond the wall sound like life itself receding from her. To move out of life, to find an inner world of imaginary truths, to escape by deliberately going mad is the game played in *More Stately Mansions*, just as Con Melody's pretenses lifts him away from the vulgar truths that press in on him from all sides.

O'Neill's characters surely chart his own way of being, and it is perhaps not too much to suggest that the Cycle was itself an elaborate daydream, and that O'Neill shut himself in his study much as Abigail shut herself in her summer house losing herself by telling romantic stories about the French Court. Another way of saying this is that the characters in the Cycle are extravagantly clad versions of the figures that really haunted O'Neill's imagination—those of himself and his family, and that the Cycle was a dark mirror that enabled O'Neill to get where he needed finally to be—to the autobiographical plays.

Working long, hard, but somewhat listlessly on the Cycle, was he fending off the truth that remained to be told? The Cycle's similarity in many specific respects to the final autobiographical works—in character, technique, situation and theme—need not be detailed. There is the outline of James Tyrone in Con Melody, of Mary Tyrone in both Nora and Deborah, of Edmund in Simon, and, perhaps, Jamie in aspects of Sara. Enough similarity exists to suggest that in writing the works of historical fiction he was somehow caught between the gray reflection of himself and the reality that thrust itself urgently forward in his memory. Was the Cycle a way of disguising a truth which he ultimately gained the courage to present? Caught between dream and reality, writing the Cycle became far too labored. Like Simon, he may have lost the self-discipline to keep himself whole and gone wandering in "the blind alley of his mind." Only after the autobiographical works were complete, did he turn back to the Cycle and finish *A Touch of the Poet*. And that, to all extents and purposes, was the end of the matter.

In her diary entry for April 29, 1954, as she thought back on her husband's final years, Mrs. O'Neill wrote:

Return to reading diaries from 1928—. Reading them now clears up so many things,—illness—not being able to work (that was the real tragedy) worry about his children's behavior, money—nervous always—taking too heavy sedation—all this piled up—& became a mixture with real heartache,—& the imaginative, tragic, dramatic mind of the artist—he finally got to the place it was impossible to separate the dream and the reality!"

And she adds "Poor darling."

III

In a Wider Context

O'Neill in The West
The Wimp in the Shower
E.G.O. vs Shav
O'Neill, the Boyg

O'Neill in the West

californians display a sentiment toward their State which to residents from beyond its borders can only appear as an irrational passion. Its fruits, flowers, ocean, industries, architecture are subjects of hymn-like devotion. Even its writers are adored, sometimes out of all proportion to their worth. Jack London is a cult figure. Robert Louis Stevenson, who dropped in on his way to the South Seas is, by Californians accounted to be a Native Son. They have not forgotten William Saroyan. They even manage to whip up enthusiasm for Robinson Jeffers. Yet it comes as a surprise to many Californians to learn that, by their definition of the term, Eugene O'Neill was a California writer. In their minds O'Neill is to be identified almost entirely with the gaunt coast of New England or the shabbier reaches of Manhattan. He has little to do with the cult of the artichoke, the surfable ocean, or any of the carefully preserved history of gold miners and cannibalistic Sierra crossings.

Yet O'Neill lived among them for eight years, from 1936 to 1944—years that were the most significantly productive in his career. In California, he wrote *Long Day's Journey into Night, A Moon for the Misbegotten, The Iceman Cometh, Hughie,* and most of *A Tale of Possessors Self-dispossessed,* the Cycle his illness forced him to destroy. It is true that little of the western world is reflected in the completed plays, but if the Cycle had been finished, O'Neill's stage would have made more of the California scene. Four of those plays were to be set in the western United States. *The Calms of Capricorn,* the play that was to follow *More Stately Mansions,* was to describe a voyage around the Horn and, as its surviving scenario reveals, it was to climax with the entrance of a clip-

Read to the American Society for Theatre Research, San Francisco, 1978 and Modern Language Association, Philadelphia, 1979.

per ship through San Francisco's Golden Gate in the year 1858. The following play, *The Earth is the Limit*, was set in San Francisco between 1858 and 1860. The action of its sequel, *Nothing is Lost Save Honor*, moved between Washington D.C., New York City, and San Francisco in the years 1860 and 1870. Subsequently, The *Man on Iron Horseback* was to be concerned with the development of the trans-continental railroad in the period between 1876 and 1893.

O'Neill's arrival in California was in a measure accidental. In 1936, he found himself dissatisfied with Casa Genotta, his newly built residence on Sea Island, Georgia. Georgia had proved a difficult place to work. The heat was often intense; there were flies, mosquitoes, and noisy cicadas; friends of his neighbor, a member of a flying club, buzzed the neighbor's house when they arrived for a visit and wished to be picked up at the airport. O'Neill's work was taxing. Although *Ah, Wilderness!* had almost written itself, he had fought *Days Without End* through many drafts. After its failure on the stage, he had started to work on the Cycle, only to see it develop in plan from a trilogy to an eleven play chronicle of staggering proportion. In 1934, his health began to deteriorate, and he was advised to stop writing for a time. A move from Georgia became desirable.

He had made friends with Sophus Keith Winther and his wife, Eline. Winther was a professor of English at the University of Washington in Seattle. His book on O'Neill had pleased its subject, and his novels of the hard lives of Danish immigrants in the Dakota territory interested both the O'Neills. Carlotta, herself of Danish origin, was drawn to the Danish professor. Thus it was that in 1936, freeing himself for a time from the problems of writing at Casa Genotta, he accepted an invitation to visit Seattle, where the Winthers would see to their comfort and where O'Neill could find material for *The Man on Iron Horseback*.

They arrived in Seattle in early November, and on November 12 rumor became reality: O'Neill was awarded the Nobel Prize for Literature. The press made the visit uncomfortable, and the O'Neills determined to escape and travel south as inconspicuously as possible to the San Francisco Bay area.

There were reasons for coming there. Carlotta Monterey had begun life as Hazel Tharsing in Oakland California. Her mother, whom O'Neill had never met, and her daughter, whom he knew and liked, lived there still. The O'Neills came to San Francisco, and almost at once—the day after Christmas—O'Neill was stricken with appendicitis and entered Merritt Hospital in Oakland.

His illness was severe. Post-operative complications were to keep him in the hospital until March, giving Carlotta time to search for a new home in a better climate than Georgia offered. She went east in January to sell Casa Genotta and upon her return began to oversee the construction of their new home in the hills above the small town of Danville, about an hour's drive east of San Francisco.

In the first years of their life together, the O'Neills had thought casually of coming to California. In a letter of April 27, 1928, from a villa in Biarritz, O'Neill had written to Kenneth Macgowan that California might prove a desirable place to live. He and Carlotta had extensive travel plans:

Our plans after the end of summer are not fixed yet. We'll probably go to Germany for a while, get married there (if Agnes does the right thing) then to England, then to South Africa for the winter (I've always wanted to go there) and up as far in the interior as Lake Tanganyika, with a permanent house in Durban, Natal (where I once touched as a sailor) where I'll write another play. Then in the spring up the opposite (East coast) to Suez and the Mediterranean—then in Greece for six months and on the Bosphorus where I'll write another drama—or maybe all this time on "Sea-Mother's Son" (keep this title to yourself!)—then stopping at India, to Hong Kong where I'll do more writing and finally, two years from this Spring, back to California where C. and I expect to make our home for good. Of course there may be changes in this itinerary....

Changes there were. O'Neill, here sounding like a breathless Somerset Maugham with touches of Phileas Fogg, was merely daydreaming. He and Carlotta did journey to the Far East in September, ready to luxuriate in their freedom, but the voyage proved disastrous, and India, Africa, and Greece were unvisited. His reference to a residence in California was only the insubstantial finale of a dream walking.

More definitive was Carlotta's view of California in a letter she wrote to Macgowan in February, 1934:

We won't go to California. I loathe the place—always have. Geographically it is marvellous (particularly north of St. Barbara!!!) but the people (generally speaking) drive me mad.—I never drank, played bridge or golf—and loathe country clubs,—so that does not make for popularity.—But I have motored over nearly every foot of that pesky state & know some lovely spots. My mother, daughter & I own a lot of real estate there.—I wish to Heaven times would get better so we could sell it.

What O'Neill knew about California before he came to live there is not easily determined with precision. His father had been a fixture of theatrical stock in San Francisco in the 1870's, and his brother Jamie had been born there in 1878. Eugene had memories of being sick in bed in San Francisco as a child when he was taken there on tour with his father, and he had been briefly in California in 1909. In that year he was rusticated following his marriage to Kathleen Jenkins by being sent to Honduras to work in a mining concern there. He shipped from Benicia, a town at the Sacramento River delta that had once threatened to rival San Francisco as the Bay's chief port. There is no record of a response on his part to the north Bay town or anything else the region had to offer.

He came west again in 1912 as a super in his father's vaudeville version of *Monte Cristo*. His biographers do not indicate that he came to San Francisco, although the tour was booked in vaudeville on the Orpheum Circuit whose western hub was the Bay city. It is certain that he went through Utah and to Colorado, perhaps absorbing through the train window some notion of what western scenery was like. The fact that it was written with vaudeville production in mind suggests that there may be a connection between this trip and his first play *A Wife for a Life*, which is laid in the Arizona desert.

The sketch, which he wrote in 1913, the year following the tour, requires *"A plain dotted with sagebrush and a lonely butte is outlined, black and sinister, against the lighter darkness of a sky with stars."* Add a few pieces of mining equipment and the setting is complete, Any amateur could create it. William S. Hart films, illustrations in *The Saturday Evening Post,* or a novel by Zane Grey would be sufficient source. But there is in the sense that the butte is "sinister," and in the precise differentiation between the darkness of the earth and the lighter darkness of the sky the possibility of a tenuous memory which the young O'Neill retained.

His next western venture was *Where the Cross is Made* (1918) and *Gold* (1920), its four-act development. Both are set on the California coast. The one-act version requires a lookout at the top of a house on "a high point of land on the California coast." "Frisco" is mentioned; the year of the action is 1900. However, the Robert Louis Stevenson adventure tale of buried treasure and ghosts that haunt a mad sea captain makes little use of its locale. Since madness is his subject, O'Neill turns the action inward to take advantage of the psychological thrills insanity offered.

Gold is a different matter. Now, the effort of the characters to set sail for the island in the Malay Archipelago where the gold was buried forms the center of the play's action. The final scene takes place in a captain's walk identical to that specified for the one-act version, but the earlier acts show what O'Neill felt California to be like. In the third act, he presents the exterior of the house, facing left toward the harbor. The house has a porch fronted by columns and windows with heavy green shutters, closed and barred. It is a Mannon mansion in embryo. To get to the sea from the house, the characters cross to the edge of a cliff and go down to the beach by a ladder. It is a clumsy set at best. The actors presumably must, once they approach the wings, climb down a ladder into a stage trap and into the sub-stage area.

Even with such awkward elaboration, the setting is geographically murky. The cliff is said to overlook a harbor and a wharf where a schooner, ready to sail, is anchored. It is, one assumes, a deep water port, for sailors appear, speaking bracing nautical one-liners like "There's a bit o' fair breeze," or "If he don't shake a leg we'll miss the tide." There is really not much of a hurry, for a sailor—as the action attests—can descend the cliff, board the ship and cast off in a single page of dialogue. Another page and the ship has "passed the p'int—and now—headin' her out to sea—so'east by east. By God, that be the course I charted fer her!"

"South-east by east"? From the West Coast? Some skipper! The ship is supposed to founder in the Indian Ocean, but with that course there is little doubt that she came aground in an artichoke patch near Monterey.

But this is not the only puzzle. If it be asked just where there is such a harbor as O'Neill describes, the answer is not a ready one. San Francisco is mentioned twice in the play, but its direction from the house is not specified. The Captain is an ex-whaler, and it is true that whaling was an industry on the Pacific Coast until the 1870's. There were once whaling stations at Monterey and Sausalito, but the latter town is within San Francisco Bay and at Monterey, the high cliffs are missing. To the north of San Francisco, except for a few river mouths, there are no deep water bays where a ship can pull to a wharf and yet be round a point and out of sight in short order. The dog-hole schooners that hauled lumber, tan bark and hides down the coast loaded offshore and had no such harbors—as their continual shipwrecks attested.

It is not, perhaps, much of a mystery. The play's second act is laid inside the wharf shed on the dock. The significant feature of the setting is at the back where a large double doorway looks over the end of the wharf to the harbor and the open sea beyond. Double doorways may be a standard feature of boat sheds, but the one O'Neill knew at first hand was the one in the shed on the wharf at Provincetown, Massachusetts, where his first plays were produced, and whose essential features he reproduced in at least one other short play, *The Rope.* Writing for the Provincetown Players, he kept to the spaces they could use quickly and efficiently, but in moving his action to California, he transferred not only the interior but the exterior geography.

The California setting is a Stevensonian fillip, chosen primarily because it was closer to the Malay Archipelago where the treasure on which the story turns was buried. This perhaps made the play's time scheme easier to deal with than did a long voyage around the Cape of Good Hope that would have been necessary from the East coast. Yet the schooner is wrecked in the Indian Ocean, *west* of the Malay Archipelago. To say the least, its course was erratic. The truth is, of course, that that countryside with its Mannon-style houses complete with Captain's Walk, the special harbor facilities, where one sails east in order to go west and approaches the Malay Peninsula through the Indian Ocean—that is New England. O'Neill's California is somewhere around Cape Cod.

O'Neill did better with his next western venture, the dream of California that sends Simeon and Peter Cabot away from their farm to seek their fortune. In *Desire Under the Elms,* the idea of California is an image—of gold in the west, linked poetically with the setting sun and a woman's golden hair—that of Jenn, Simeon's dead wife. The California of this play is poetically conceived, not unlike the idea of the South Seas in *Mourning Becomes Electra*—an object of longing that contrasts with repressive realities.

The west as a dream, the idea of a golden California, proved to be his final recorded use of the far west. In the complex, contorted scenario of *The Calms of Capricorn* the California gold fields form a major thematic concept, counterpointing the imagery of the sea as an element in man's fate. In this strange play, the widowed Sara Melody Harford, who had first appeared in *A Touch of the Poet,* and her sons, Ethan, Jonathan, Wolfe and Honey journey to California on the clipper ship, *"Dream of the West."* It is a randy Ship of Fools. Becalmed while trying to set a record run from Boston to San Francisco, the clipper becomes something like a brothel as a whorish sensualist named Leda Cade seduces the majority of the male members of the cast. Her doctrine is simple, if grossly, put:

> What else is [love but bodies?]...Bodies are all right, aren't they— healthy and natural. Aren't we animals? Can you go to bed with a soul? Poetic drivel aside, love may start in heaven but it goes on or it dies in bed.

Sexual possession is linked with the desire for material possession, bodily love and greed are combined in a series of quickly intercut scenes, almost cinematic in their rhythm. Leda's sexuality is linked thematically with the sea. As the play's central character, Ethan Harford, says to his mother:

> I want nothing. It is what I need that I must have—must & will have—and will gladly pay the world for.... Victory over the sea—and so freedom & rebirth. I speak to you in symbols which neither of us can think but which our hearts understand, because I love you and because I love and hate the sea, which you can understand, being also a mother. For the sea is the mother of life—is a woman of all moods for all men—all seductive & evil—devil, mother or mistress or daughter or water-front drab—and it is as a sign and symbol of freedom to me that someday as captain of a ship I shall fight her storms and calms and fogs and cross-currents and capricious airs and make a faster voyage around the Horn to the Golden Gate than ever man has made—as a last gesture of victory, now

when the era of American triumph over the sea is dying from the money panic of the greedy earthbound.

In the scenario, O'Neill is evidently thinking his way not only through the narrative and the characters, but through the theme as well. Ethan's words are an exploration of the motives of the play's protagonist, and mark O'Neill's attempt to define the major images that would ultimately comprise the whole meaning of the play and perhaps of the Cycle. The theme of the greedy earthbound, expressed in sexual symbolism, had been more definitively worked through in *More Stately Mansions,* but in the sequel, the additional elements of the sea and the Golden Gate brought complexity and not a little ambiguity

Quite possibly, O'Neill would have clarified the thematic ambiguities in *The Calms of Capricorn* and *More Stately Mansions* as he did in the one completed Cycle play, *A Touch of the Poet.* His thrust was toward simplicity of statement and staging, but it took him time—often years—to achieve the cleanly wrought dramatic style of the plays he finished at Tao House. All that can be assumed from the scenario is that he saw the west as somehow intertwined with the materialistic motifs of the sea and sex, as a force to be conquered and possessed before it could defeat its would-be possessors.

O'Neill kept the idea of the west as a materialistic Mecca throughout the action of the shipboard scenes. In the ship's steerage there is a crowd of men heading for the gold fields. Unseen, they serve as chorus to the play, singing "Sacramento" and other miners' songs almost unceasingly. Like the fog horn in *Long Day's Journey into Night* or the native chant in *The Moon of the Caribbees* or the drums in *The Emperor Jones,* the gold-seeker's song preys on the nerves of the characters. At times, as a way of indicating the linking of the themes of the sea and the dream of gold, O'Neill called for the gold-seeker's song to blend with and war against a sea chanty: *"As a background is the triumphant song of the gold-seekers, dominating a subdued, beaten sea-chanty."* The music is a continual hymn to a betraying dream. O'Neill notes of the singers that "their leader had heard from a brother in Cal. of big new strike and he'd gotten company of poor neighbors—it will be like first days [i.e. 1849, six years before the play's action]—poor things I hope they have better luck than those others, that this wonderful strike isn't just a fairy tale."

The dream of California and its gold is a delusion. The west proves to be a place where a man's dreams are "knocked out of his head." It becomes in the end nothing more than a politician's promise when Honey Harford—who will become the politician protagonist of *Nothing is Lost Save Honor*—turns the dream to his advantage, promising the gold-seekers as they enter the Golden Gate:

> There's land, the Golden Gate, and behind it is hills full of gold—I promise you you'll all be rich—and you know me, Honey Harford, my word is as good as my bond.... I promise you I'll see you get everything your heart desires tomorrow.

The play was to end as *"The Dream of the West"* entered the Golden Gate, and as Ethan and his partner in love and crime, Nancy, commit suicide by giving themselves to the sea. California remained only at the edge of the play's vision.

And that was the sum of the impact of the west on O'Neill's plays. The house he built in California is in some detail a hacienda-like ranch house, but the orient, not the west, gave the house its name, Tao House, and it was designed to shut the western country-side from sight. High walls surround the garden and, although the site commands a spectacular view of Mount Diablo, the windows take little advantage of it. O'Neill's study is isolated and dark, and there he turned away from the California world to explore his past and the memories of New England and New York where inescapably his truth lay.

The Wimp in the Shower

D evoted as I am to this nation's pursuit of the grotesque and the ugly and enthusiastically committed to its belief in insatiable greed, I sometimes turn on the television to discover the newest variations on these venerable American themes. The act is a form of patriotic self-torture, but an hour's masochism, now and then, sometimes raises curious speculation about our national identity as it is defined in the behavior of the archetypal role models brought before our wondering, but often drowsy eyes.

In particular, in recent months, I have been struck by a figure who seems so at odds with the creation that comes most readily to mind when the American male is mentioned—that figure so indelibly defined by the heroic John Wayne clones on film—that some comment seems necessary, if only to break the stunned silence that greets his every appearance.

I became aware of him first in a detergent commercial. He stood in a shower, showing a bare, but decorously unmuscled right shoulder. Although it was to be presumed that he had finished his ablutions, he was not particularly damp or dripping. Physically, that is. Spiritually it was another matter.

His wife, a woman of resolute charm, hands him a towel. Our man's first response is not to use, but to smell it.

"It's dirty," he tells his wife.

She, with the common sense of bright women everywhere, answers, "How can you tell. It's brown."

He offers it to her to smell, and she, convinced, rushes to the laundry to wash it, leaving our hero to make the best of life in a stall

---

Presented at a meeting of the Modern Language Association, San Francisco, 1984.

---

shower so small that in it even Superman would have trouble changing his leotards.

We are evidently at a far remove from Superman, if not from Clark Kent. The wimp in the shower deserves the pneumonia he has wished upon himself, but he is neither the first nor the last of his breed. Cloned hundreds of times, he stands as an exhibition of tolerable and therefore emulatable manhood. He carries out superstrong trash bags; he gropes myopically in his medicine chest for Alka Seltzer; he exults when his dishwashing liquid gets his glassware "lemony;" he welcomes us to "The World of Heartburn"; he wakes his wife in the small hours, demanding "new improved" Nyquil or a similar analgesic; he eats TWIX; and he adores cookies with peculiar names and, again, "new, improved" flavor.

I am not sure—it is a very long time back—who the role models were who defined the American male in my formative years. Modest, gallant Lindbergh played a part in our consciousness then. Will Rogers had force and Johnny Weismuller as Tarzan was important, as were Tom Mix and the young Gary Cooper. And one remembers the F. Scott Fitzgerald suavité of the gentleman wearing Arrow Collars, and the nation's almost mythical strong man, Charles Atlas, who was once a 97-pound weakling. Today, I suspect, if one were to ask a representative cross-section of Americans to define their idea of an American hero, the result would be a composite of Eastwood, Stallone, and Schwarzenegger, with a sprinkling of politicians and sports professionals. A touch or two of urbanity might be added, but there would be no crippling displays of intellectual power or especial talent, other than to downshift a Porsche and to say "Gee" to a horse.

Yet, if you look for this equestrian statue on stage or in real life, you discover him to be an increasingly vanishing breed. On television, with jingling spurs and with revolvers undulating at his hips, he bursts through saloon doors, stalks to the bar, and orders a 7-Up. A group of what appear to be the world's toughest athletes at that most masculine of hang-outs, a saloon bar, jovially give one another blindfold taste-tests of beer or burst into choric song as if they had been rehearsing *Naughty Marietta* during half-time. These days, you see the macho hero in magazines posing in pastel-colored jockey shorts, or, again without his pants, brooding about Kent cigarettes.

Wimps are everywhere. Chinese fashion, we might designate this year as "The Year of the Wimp." Even in the most vigorous of contemporary video series, you will have noticed that there is, in addition to the stalwart hero or heroine, a wimpish sidekick. Some are disguised by the padding in the shoulders of their suits and their ingratiating hairstyling. Is his name Pierce Brosnan? Or Dudley Moore? More normally, now that Tonto and others of his kind have gone out of ethnic fashion, there rides unabashed alongside the Last of the Stalwarts, the silly cohort, the sexless man, the fool, the apparently essential antidote to machosis.

Where did he come from and why is he so evident as to rank as a cultural phenomenon? For one thing, the wimp is not threatening. As a salesman on video, he never grabs your lapels or sticks his foot in the door of your awareness. He is off-hand, self-deprecating, and, in theory at least, a little funny. His is the softest of sells. He does not threaten his listener with rational argument, but rather sets a comic example when, in need of Alka Selzer or Nyquil, he pretends urgent pain and calls upon our sympathy at the same time as he tries to evoke our laughter.

The melding of laughter and sympathy provides a clue to his success both in television and in the theatre. He is a comic figure, and it is in comedy that he has made his most memorable and durable appearances. He goes a long way back. From the early days of films, he has been a type of protagonist that public has loved. The baby-faced, simpering Harry Langdon, Harold Lloyd who played "Grandma's Boy," and a host of others in whose repertory of emotions being bashful was a primary need. George K. Arthur, John Bunny, Fatty Arbuckle, Eddie

Cantor, Woody Allen, Gene Wilder, Peter Sellers, even—at moments—Keaton and Chaplin. Sometimes they came in pairs: Wheeler and Woolsey, for example, and as a sort of apotheosis, Laurel and Hardy. Other, more aggressive comedians had little to do with wimpishness. W. C. Fields ate wimps for breakfast, and the Marx Brothers early on dropped Zeppo, the male ingenue, from their team. But with Fields and the Marxes as exceptions, it seems undeniable that America has had a long love affair with the milquetoasts of stage and screen.

Inevitably, as the figure became a recognizable stereotype, a traditional, partly mythic story attached to him. American legend has it that the meek shall inherit the kingdom, that the unknown immigrant shall rise and prosper, that the country innocent shall by his own virtue and manly acumen become head of the Horatio Alger Corporation. In comedy, the narrative form of the wimp story bears resemblance to this legend. He is usually set in a context where he is alien among characters who are physically stronger, richer, more sophisticated, and more dishonest than he. He is the butt of any joke or con game, the victim of any trap or assault, a scapegoat, a good-natured fall guy. He comes often from the country to the Big City, and his situation sets in opposition rural and urban America. Country people are naïve, but often straitlaced, puritanical, suspicious—except for the girl who is pretty and obsessively faithful to the wimp. City people, on the other hand, are freewheeling, easy-living, often broke, unscrupulous, sexy, cynical and shallow. The wimp, usually, feels held down by the limits of country living and strives for something better by going to the city. There he is caught up in an enterprise such as movie-making. horse-racing, play-producing, athletics, song-writing. The action in which the wimp is involved leads him by a devious trail of error to a lucky triumph and the arms of the girl he left behind.

The lucky wimp was a favorite hero of George S. Kaufman and his collaborators, who played endless variations on the story. *Merton of the Movies,* dramatized from the novel by Harry Leon Wilson, set the pattern early. Merton, a small-time grocery clerk, is a devoted reader of screen magazines. He takes a correspondence course in screen acting and heads for Hollywood, where his ineptitude makes him a leading actor in farce comedies. There is no more to it than that, yet the play has succeeded out of hand and been filmed three times, the last with Red Skelton, a specialist in wimp depiction.

Kaufman's first collaboration with Moss Hart, *Once in a Lifetime* was essentially a re-working of *Merton of the Movies* with the naïf (this time from New York) triumphing in Hollywood as a producer by dumb luck. Kaufman has a reputation as a satirist, but the satiric tone that proclaims that all Hollywood people are idiots is a thin veneer over a sentimental story, not of virtue triumphant, but of naïveté winning out over pseudo-sophistication.

He repeated the story in *June Moon,* his collaboration with Ring Lardner. Fred, the country song writer, achieves fortune and a happy marriage by writing songs of incredible banality:

> June Moon shining above
> Will my true love come soon?
> June Moon I am so blue;
> I know you long for her, too.

He reversed the formula (city wimp goes to the country) in *George Washington Slept Here*, and framed it in a domestic setting in *Dulcy* where, for once, the wimp was female—not an idea that caught on.

Many of Kaufman's contemporaries have used the formula— Erwin Trowbridge, the greeting card poet in *Three Men on a Horse* by John Cecil Holm and George Abbott, or Leo Davis, the playwright-protagonist of *Room Service* by John Murray and Alan Boretz belong to the club. There are many more.

It is perhaps of interest that a number of these ineffectual naïfs are in some way associated with the arts, often with some kind of poetry. Their artistic talents lend warmth to an otherwise banal emptiness. Art suggests a modicum of sensitivity and provides a capability that can lead to success. The naïf is, of course, never a serious artist, but he does well with what he has and is somehow redeemed by having in him "the touch of a poet."

But what of his opposite number? Is there a tragic wimp also "touched with poetry?" Eugene O'Neill first used the phrase "touch of the poet" in 1920 to describe Robert Mayo, the ineffectual poetic dreamer of Beyond the Horizon:

[Robert Mayo] is a tall, slender young man of twenty-three. There is a touch of the poet about him expressed in his high forehead and wide, dark eyes. His features are delicate and refined, leaning to weakness in the mouth and chin.

His brother is his manly opposite:

[Andrew Mayo] is twenty-seven years old, an opposite type to Robert—husky, sun-bronzed, handsome in a large-featured, manly fashion—a son of the soil, intelligent in a shrewd way, but with nothing of the intellectual about him.

The brothers set in frame the theatrical concepts of American manhood. Andrew would have made out all right at the O.K. Corral, but Robert brought into focus the sensitive weak-willed victim of circumstances and self whose failure of will makes him incapable of coping with even the routines of daily life, much less with a significant destiny. He is the embodiment of the tragic wimp.

Throughout the twentieth century American drama, the figure of which Robert Mayo is a prototype recurs so frequently in both the tragic and the comic theatres that one might hold him to be this country's favorite protagonist. Mr. Zero of Elmer Rice's *The Adding Machine,* John Howard Lawson's expressionist creation, Roger Bloomer, O'Neill's Dion Anthony, Alan Squier in Robert Sherwood's *The Petrified Forest,* Ned Seton in Barry's *Holiday,* Kilroy, Brick Pollitt, and Chance Wayne, a trio by Tennessee Williams, and even Arthur Miller's Willy Loman are paralleled by the Freds, Harolds, Mertons and Clarences of the comic scene.

Although he rarely shows courage or even much will to endure, and although he cries out against life without attempting to master it, turning himself into a ready victim, the tragic wimp, like his bumbling but lucky comic counterpart is still a figure for whom it is easy to muster sympathy. The wimp is so put upon, so beaten down, so knocked about, so beset by bad luck that his audience almost inevitably finds him moving or amusing. The comic version is an easy creation; the tragic figure is never fully tragic. Arthur Miller, casting unintentional light on the central critical problem of *Death of a Salesman,* once wrote that "when pathos is finally derived" in a play—when the fullest, ultimate emotion of the play is only one of pathetic sympathy—the play falls short of tragedy. This is true even of *Death of a Salesman.* When the protagonist is so limp, one tends to become a scoutmaster, crying "Stand up straight! Stiffen the lip! Forward march!" Since luck plays so large a part in his destiny, there are always options which the soft-shelled protagonist fails (or is not allowed by the playwright) to explore. Noël Coward irreverently remarked that he didn't know what all the fuss was about in Willy Loman's household. After all, he pointed out, Willy was sitting on a prime piece of New York real estate. He could have sold it for thousands.

There is a certain falsity in both the tragic and comic American protagonist. The comic story lies: it says that stupidity will conquer all, bringing clowns to consummately happy weddings and fancy bank accounts. It is a happy lie, rather like the old melodramatic concept of

"Virtue Triumphant" over foreclosed mortgages, menacing buzz saws and attempted rape. It has been as pleasing to American theatres as the concept of poetic justice was to the eighteenth century theatre-goer. It perfects nature with an untruth: Blessed are the spineless; they shall know success!

The quasi-tragic depictions are also lies, in the sense that they make failure inevitable. The portrait of the tragic wimp denies the American dream by substituting a nightmare: materialistic society destroys sensitive poetic souls. Such a poor creature will never grow up to be President, own two cars, belong to the country club and march forward to a significant future. But, in the denial of the "dream," the dramatists may have presented a theoretical "reality" as false as the dream. It is probably safe to say that American males don't snivel. At least not so long and so often as these tragic protagonists do.

The drama of a country during a given era in its accumulated impact creates a generalized picture of the society that has produced it, a society which the stage in its turn helps to define. The stage takes the leading elements of the society—realities, fictions, desires, beliefs—and transmutes them in simplified terms so that audiences see themselves and in part model themselves after what they see on stage. What the prevalence of the wimpish hero means is a matter that can be debated along with the presence of his antithesis who marches boldly to his destiny along the deserted streets of a cow-town. The wimp's presence suggests a failure of nerve, a withdrawal into a shell to shut out the rough, jangling experience of this country's wide-open growth during the twentieth century. But this is a problem for more detailed analysis than is possible here. It is perhaps sufficient to the present purpose to point out the prevalence in the American theatre of the wimpish figure and his pairing with the aggressively macho figure who stalks the screen, and to suggest that trapped in every Charles Atlas there is a 97-pound weakling crying to be freed.

E.G.O. vs. Shav*

The position of Eugene O'Neill in the thematic context of the American theatre is central. Just as Bernard Shaw proved responsive to the major currents of his theatre and reshaped its uses for his purposes, and as Shakespeare took from and returned to his theatre many motifs, themes, characters and techniques, so O'Neill stood as a lens, a central reflector of the theatre in America in the twentieth century.

As an artist of influence, his life began in 1916, when the Provincetown Players produced his short play, *Bound East for Cardiff*, which he had written two years earlier. With posthumous productions and significant revivals, he has continued to dominate the American stage until the present, sixty years later. In his lifetime he completed drafts of sixty-two plays. Eleven were destroyed, and several exist in unpublished and unproduced typescripts. Some are short plays, but others are dramas of marathon length. No playwright in English, except Shaw and Shakespeare, has worked so steadily, so long and so seriously. Like the two British playwrights, O'Neill began work at a moment when his theatre was taking its characteristic form, and, like them, he defined its shape by showing his contemporaries the potential of the themes and conventions that were the theatre's available materials. Shakespeare's treatment of the revenge formula in *Hamlet*, Shaw's development of the domestic-triangle plot in *Candida* are matched by

---

In 1949, Shaw wrote a puppet play entitled Shakes vs. Shav *in which he caused the two playwright-puppets to argue their merits. My title is borrowed from Shaw's in order to match the two major dramatists writing in English in this century.*

Reprinted by permission of Methuen Co., Ltd. from The Revels History of the Drama in English, *vol. viii. [London, 1977]*

O'Neill's work with, for example, the American folk play in *Desire Under the Elms*. Shaw and Shakespeare occasionally nodded and at times O'Neill was staggeringly inept. Yet the greatness of which each was capable justified and fulfilled the purposes of his theatre by pulling together into a coherent system of thought and attitude the elements of which lesser writers used only fragments.

O'Neill's first play that can be seen as fully characteristic of the American theatre was a work that emerged more than by accident than design. *Bound East for Cardiff* was one of several inexpert, mannered short plays of no value, written at the outset of his career. Unlike its companions, it is authentic O'Neill and a play of a genuinely American stamp. Its scene is the seaman's forecastle on a tramp freighter, sailing from New York to Cardiff. Its action is an encounter between Yank, who is dying of an injury, and his friend Driscoll. For most of the action, the scene is left to the two men, who speak of the friendship that has emerged during their rough life together and of a dream each has held, but of which neither has spoken earlier, of leaving the sea and of finding a farm inland, where they can become something more than the ocean's nomads. At the end of the play Yank dies, and the dream is lost, but the play offers the suggestion that in the shared confessional the men have touched one another and in so doing have justified their existence. O'Neill also suggests that the two, like all those who go to sea, become the sea's children and are held by the sea's power as if they were in thrall to a god.

From this small beginning O'Neill moved forward, trying many styles and subjects, but essentially developing the idea that men sought two goals, the truth of their own natures and the special essence of a force to which they could "belong." In *Beyond the Horizon* he defined the nature of that search more fully as he told of Robert Mayo's restless desire to go to sea and of his destruction when he tries to serve the land to which he does not belong. At the time of its successful first production in 1920, the only play to which it could conveniently be compared was William Vaughn Moody's *The Great Divide* (1907), a play whose conflict centers on the cultural differences between the refined eastern Americans and the roughneck westerners. *Beyond the Horizon* announced firmly the new themes that were to dominate the plays of rural life thereafter. Mayo is the restless, poetic hero out of place in his surroundings, a prototype that was to prove for O'Neill and for many of his contemporaries a congenial alter ego. His dream of going to sea and of finding exotic lands beyond the horizon is the first statement of the dream motif, the search for an earthly paradise that others were to use repeatedly. The inability of Mayo to respond to the force moving in the earth again anticipates the view of the power of the land that will prevail in plays of rural life. O'Neill's implication, more philosophically complete than the ruminations of later dramatists, is that all men belong to a large, elemental force, which they must serve as if they are serving a god. They are possessed by its energy and power, but if for some reason they fall out of harmony, becoming dispossessed as is Mayo, when he tries to serve the land, they are doomed to a waste of their vitality. The right relationship is shown in *"Anna Christie"* in the figure of Mat Burke, who is a child of the sea, and in whom the sea's power beats fiercely. The spiritual waste is again demonstrated in Yank in *The Hairy Ape* and in Brutus in *The Emperor Jones.*

In his tragedy, *Desire Under the Elms,* O'Neill explored the relation of men and the land complexly and with clear philosophical underpinnings derived from Greek myth (Phaedra and Oedipus) and from the writings of Friedrich Nietzsche. In the conflict of Ephraim Cabot with his son Eben, and in the love story of Eben and his step-mother Abby, O'Neill wrote what was perhaps the archetypal American tragedy, the tragedy of men who belong to the land and who desire to be possessed by its power, but who are trapped into a struggle for its ownership. The land, O'Neill implies, cannot be possessed. It demands surrender. Eben desires to sink into its entity in rapture and Dionysian forgetfulness, as a man might love a woman. He desires to serve the land as its priest and its son, for O'Neill, making the connection that other dramatists have only implied, sees that the land is also a mother. Incestuously loving his stepmother is a way of loving the land, but, when he is trapped into trying to own the land, his sense of alienation and dispossession makes him bitter and potentially violent. In right relationship with the land and the woman, he is in harmony with the source of his life and comfort.

Desire Under the Elms brought together into a coherent pattern of thought the fragments that other playwrights used, and it was the capstone of the first phase of O'Neill's career. He continued to explore the lives of men seeking to belong, and in particular their search for a woman who, like a mother, will possess them and comfort them and remove the stresses of their disoriented lives. In *Strange Interlude* for example, he created in Nina Leeds the portrait of a possessive woman who feeds on the lives of all the men around her. Their desire, she says, makes her feel "whole," and she does all she can to keep them in thrall. Viewed coldly, she is monstrous but O'Neill does not look at her objectively. He casts a veil of sympathy over her, and equates her needs with the tides, the deep rhythm of the sea, the nine-month cycle of human pregnancy. She becomes like the earth, a goddess to be served.

The effect is repeated in the trilogy, *Mourning Becomes Electra,* wherein O'Neill, following the legend of Electra, tells of the conflict of Christine Mannon and her daughter Lavinia. Orin, her son, links her as an object of his desire with a dream of a tropical island paradise, and, after he has murdered her lover and driven her to suicide, he goes with his sister on a voyage to such islands. There the sister changes, taking on the mother's coloration and sensuality to become the sister-mother-lover of her brother.

Throughout O'Neill's work, the image of the desired mother sought in a surrogate woman reappears. She is to be found in Abby, the stepmother of *Desire Under the Elms,* she is the prostitute Cybel in *The Great God Brown,* and in *Dynamo* she is the cow-like May Fife, to whom the embittered hero goes for refuge from his repressive Puritan family. In his later works, the figures of mother, wife and whore are bewilderingly linked together. In Josie Hogan, the giant slut who comforts Jamie Tyrone in *A Moon for the Misbegotten,* and in the mother and daughter-in-law of *More Stately Mansions,* the figure of the mother who is a lover and of the wife who is a mother and whore are woven into patterns of possession and dispossession, which can give men salvation or lead them to their destruction.

In some plays, of course, O'Neill has it otherwise. The simple Irish peasant wife, Nora Melody of *A Touch of the Poet,* and Essie Miller, the fresh-faced guardian of her family's welfare in *Ah, Wilderness!* are two important variants on the pattern of possessive maternal force. But in the tragic counterpart of *Ah, Wilderness!, Long Day's Journey into Night,* Essie Miller becomes Mary Tyrone, a portrait of O'Neill's own mother, whose failure to act as a guardian has plunged her sons and her husband into emotionally crippling loss. Notably, in the later plays of O'Neill, the absence of the mother sends the sons to find a surrogate in incestuously oriented relationships with maternal whores, or, as with Josie Hogan, a woman who can be whore, lover, mother and goddess in one.

Like the other American dramatists whose work he anticipated and of whom he is an epitome, O'Neill turned to an examination of the failure of the American dream and to an analysis of the destruction of his country by materialistic greed. As with his treatment of the themes of the land, the mother and the lost dream, he was able to bring into a coherent pattern of meaning the elements used by others. The themes of possession and dispossession announced early in his career, which gave rise to his concerns for the mother and the land, also prompted a searching look at America's problems, forming the center of his long Cycle of plays on American historical subjects, *A Tale of Possessors Self-dispossessed.*

The Cycle was a work-in-progress, which O'Neill began about 1933 and continued until illness forced him to abandon the effort ten years later. He destroyed the scenarios and uncompleted plays in 1953, the year of his death. Two plays survive, *A Touch of the Poet,* which he completed in 1936, and an unrevised draft of the following play, *More Stately Mansions,* which was finished about 1939. When the scheme was fully developed, O'Neill had in plan eleven plays covering the course of American history from the colonial beginnings to the middle years of the Depression. It was a work of extraordinary magnitude, and, as the surviving plays indicate, would have been of the highest quality. That O'Neill could not live to complete it is a major loss to the drama not only of the United States but of the English-speaking world.

O'Neill's view of his country's failure was that greed—one of the lost plays was entitled *Greed of the Meek*—had destroyed the hopeful freedoms which the citizens of the uncharted new nation had once enjoyed. In tracing the lives of the members of an American dynasty from simple beginnings—its forebear was an Irish immigrant in the mid-eighteenth century—through two centuries of acquisitive corruption of the land, O'Neill asserted what he called the "spiritual undertheme" of the Cycle: that those who attempt to possess the earth are in the end dispossessed; that in gaining the whole world they lose their souls. It was, of course, a theme asserted by many Europeans in the years of the Depression and Second World War, but in America the theme gained especial pathos because, in the United States, what has been lost is so fresh in memory, so recent in history. The pure world of Henry David Thoreau still has reality in American minds. The genial, loving life of Tom Sawyer and Huckleberry Finn is a part of the childhood of most Americans. It does not seem to be dead. Yet, as the nation moved on to the international political scene, as labor organized itself in the face of the agonies of the Depression, as the land turned to dust in the great drought, the memory became a dream, a sentimentalized myth, and in its place there came the greedy enslaver, the hog-like, fox-like American who despoiled and enslaved and transformed his free country into a materialistic wilderness. In *More Stately Mansions* the heroine, Sara Harford, speaks for all the possessors when she tells an employee in her office, "I am good because I am strong. You are evil because you are weak."

The lament for the dream lost pervades the late plays of O'Neill and proves to be the most poignant theme of America's tragic drama. In *A Touch of the Poet* Deborah Harford speaks of the men in her family and warns her son's fiancée that the Harford men "never part with their dreams even when they deny them." In his final works O'Neill drew portraits of those who are haunted by dreams they have sought to deny. He called the dreams the "lie of the pipe dream" and made the lie the core of *The Iceman Cometh, Hughie, A Moon for The Misbegotten* and the autobiographical tragedy, *Long Day's Journey into Night.* In these plays the action is to measure present realities against a vision of what has been lost, and O'Neill held that the vision, even if it is clearly a self-deluding lie, is better than the present which man has created for himself. The down-and-outs of *The Iceman Cometh* dwell amidst the drifting recollections of the past, each withdrawn into a shell of illusion at Harry Hope's saloon which one character calls "The Bottom-of-the-Sea Rathskeller." In *Hughie,* the only remaining play of a planned cycle of one-act plays, the two characters deliberately lose themselves in an illusion which proves to be the only way either can survive.

In his autobiography, as he images his mother, father and brother, O'Neill shows himself and his parents as being able to live in the present because each has had something in the past to which they can cling. With whiskey and morphine, they try to drift away from their fog-bound cottage, into the past where each had a vision that was like "a saint's vision of beatitude." In *A Moon for the Misbegotten,* which continues the story of his brother Jamie, O'Neill created for the character a fictitious moment—a night of remorseful confession that brings forgiveness and love—that can become the memory of beatitude. Otherwise Jamie would have had no dream.

O'Neill's version of the motif of the lost dream is the fullest statement of the nostalgic clinging to the past that occupied so much of the endeavors of the American theatre in the second quarter of the century. It is no accident that his conviction of the necessity of illusion as a way to sustain life led him, well ahead of his American and European contemporaries, into an exploration of the existential world, and to the kind of play that later was to become a characteristic American drama: the two-character confessional.

The Iceman Cometh is such a play, progressing in confessional duologues and leading to Hickey's massive confession of guilt at his inability to love. Hope's saloon is a wasteland in which men huddle together, getting what warmth they can from touching one another with the endless narration of their dreams. Hughie, more clearly a formal prototype of what was to come, depicts two characters in a cheap New York hotel lobby, one talking endlessly to pass the small hours of the pre-dawn vacuum, the other speaking scarcely at all, hardly hearing and rarely responding to what is said. The voices drop into silence and spell out the existential emptiness of modern life. What saves, again, is illusion—fabricated, open illusion—eagerly accepted by both men. Roles are developed, those of the con man and his mark, the eternal sucker, and the play ends with a saving moment of contact, achieved through the medium of a fake dice game that both pretend is real. The play's lyric intensity makes it one of the true poetic dramas of the modern theatre, a work which lies, for all of its difference of subject, in the direct tradition of Synge.

The Iceman Cometh was written in 1939, Hughie in 1941, and the dates place O'Neill well in front of the later group of dramatists who seek to interpret the plight of men in a world where God was dead. The American's understanding of that plight was, in its resolution, essentially different from the statements of the French philosophical playwrights or of any of the angry outcries of the British playwrights of the 1950s. O'Neill's humanity, the desperate crying-out for blessing, sets him apart from the harder-edged European scene, but this is not to say that he was incapable of clear perception about his world or that he sentimentalized his characters without a sense of irony as he did so. In all of the late plays, the actions are set forth in such a way as to complicate and round out the central search for vision. Although they are deceptive in their length and their deliberately orchestrated repetition, the last plays are as stripped down, as uncompromising as, say, Sartre's *Huis clos* or the plays of Beckett.

Yet, in the last analysis, it is not Beckett or Sartre or Synge whom O'Neill most resembles but, oddly, Bernard Shaw. The bulk and the quality of the work by the two playwrights are sufficient to mark them as pre-eminent in the twentieth-century dramatic pantheon. Both men spoke clearly for their nation and for their time, and, although on the surface they seem as unlike one another as light and dark, the integral relationship between day and night suggests that at the source the two may have more in common than their common language.

Like O'Neill's, Shaw's works are an epitome of the drama of his time and country. He offered highly personalized versions of the Pinero and Jones triangle play in *Candida,* the melodramatic thriller in *The Devil's Disciple,* the Graustarkian romance, the drawing-room comedy, the chronicle history, the farce, and so on. At the same time, he also moved out of the currents of the popular theatre towards a more personalized kind of play that was thin in narrative, disquisitory in content and mythic in intention. In such a play as *The Simpleton of the Unexpected Isles,* Shaw appears to be writing an expressionistic play, as experimental in its way as O'Neill's theatrical experiments.

Departures from realistic dramaturgy led both men to write plays that were exceptionally long and mythic in content. It was perhaps Shaw's *Back to Methuselah,* which the Theatre Guild produced in 1922, that encouraged O'Neill to write dramas of inordinate length. Yet it is not essential to posit a direct connection between Shaw's massive statement of the myth of creative evolution and O'Neill's long choric drama, *Lazarus Laughed,* which he wrote in 1925. The two plays are attempts to frame new religious doctrine, suitable to their nations and their epochs. Both plays emerge from evolutionary conceptions. Like Shaw, O'Neill had responded creatively to conceptions that Darwin and Lamarck had loosed into modern thought. O'Neill, was no reader of scientists or philosophers, Nietzsche excepted, but had absorbed his ideas of evolution from novelists such as Jack London, Stephen Crane and Frank Norris. Both *The Emperor Jones* and *The Hairy Ape* owe much to London's novel *The Call of the Wild,* which shows how a dog released in the Alaskan wilderness returns to the savage condition of a wolf. Like the dog, the Emperor and the Ape move backwards, down the evolutionary scale, towards savagery and in *The Hairy Ape* towards ape-like Darwinian origins. The direction is diametrically opposite to that urged by Shaw, and yet the point of departure is the same. Neither playwright, faced with the consequences of evolutionary theory, was willing to exist in a world without God, and both sought to describe the nature of divinity in plays that were essentially religious. The difference in the myths each formulated lies in the direction of the search.

Back to Methuselah, like *Man and Superman* before it, points towards the upward-spiralling movement of man's evolutionary progress. The Nietzschean superman climbs forward to a point where, his Apollonian impulses fulfilled, he can leave behind all flesh and become the "whirlpool of pure intelligence" of which Lilith, the universal feminine principle, speaks at the drama's conclusion. O'Neill's superman, the risen Lazarus, also speaks of man's goal as an entry into cosmic forces, but the direction to be taken is downwards to the submerging of life in primordial matter. What men call life is death, O'Neill argued. To die is to lose the corrupting, fearful individuation of being that separates men from the cosmic processes of change and eternal growth. Only while man is conscious does he fear death and tyrannize over his fellows. "As dust," Lazarus preaches, "you are eternal change, and everlasting growth...." The loss of consciousness, the end of thought, the disappearance into the whirlpool of matter are for O'Neill the supreme good.

The differences between the two dramatists in their systems of value, their philosophical vision and their temperament are myriad, yet there is a radical similarity in their work. For example, one sees woman as the creative, life-giving evolutionary force, the pursuing Everywoman, Lilith, St. Joan, goading men to higher achievement. To the other, woman is the womb, the center of quiet, the sought, the betrayer, the source of lost vision and destroyed dream. Yet both dramatists feel that woman stands near the philosophical center of life, and that men circle around the force she radiates.

In Shaw, the Irish heritage is loquacious, witty, styled with careful, eloquent rhetoric. In O'Neill, the black Irish urge is towards folk poetry, rhapsodic in its repetition. Both playwrights, it has been said, talk too much. Yet, in the theatre, they create a dialogue entirely appropriate to the tone, texture and meaning of what they present, and it is speech that cannot be entirely evaluated on the page. Certainly no other playwrights in English in this century have so consistently fired their audiences. As masters of theatrical techniques, these two, alone since the death of Shakespeare, have continually filled theatres and have had a steady record of successful revivals.

Interestingly, once both playwrights had become established in their countries, they came under the sponsorship of the New York Theatre Guild, so that they stood, as it were, side by side before American audiences. In the history of the English-speaking theatre, the conjunction of two such major playwrights, working steadily from season to season under the sign of a single producing organization, cannot be duplicated except in the Globe Theatre, when Shakespeare and Jonson were at the peak of their careers.

To envisage a meeting of the two is not quite possible. Shaw called O'Neill "a fantee Shakespeare who peoples his isles with Calibans," and no doubt O'Neill appeared something of a monster to the ascetic Irishman. Yet Shaw understood much about O'Neill. Hearing that the American had given up drinking, Shaw commented that he would probably never again write a good play. Happily, he was wrong, and O'Neill's greatest work lay ahead of that moment. Yet Shaw's comment reveals that he understood O'Neill's Irish turn towards darkness and fantee madness. For his part, O'Neill had found much in Shaw's work that was of formative importance. His reading of *The Quintessence of Ibsenism* had led him as a young man to the work of Ibsen and to other masters of late nineteenth-century thought. Like Shaw he was greatly influenced by Nietzsche, although his reading to the German philosopher was highly selective and fed less on the intellectual substance in Nietzschean doctrine than on the emotional coloration of the writing.

Nietzsche's differentiation between the Apollonian and Dionysian modes of perception conveniently points towards the difference between the two playwrights, at the same time as it suggests the radical connection. It may be said that, in the plays of Shaw, the highest, most compelling action is the education of the characters, an education that causes them to move towards a higher, more conscious plane of being. It is an Apollonian motion. In O'Neill, the movement is Dionysian—towards the rapturous immersion of the conscious self into a center of life-energy that is eternal and unchanging. Shaw is movement; O'Neill is stasis. Shaw is consciousness; O'Neill forgetfulness. Shaw is thought; O'Neill is memory. Shaw is ascetic; O'Neill is drunken. Shaw is visionary; O'Neill dreams. Shaw seeks life; O'Neill seeks to lose it. What is not true is that Shaw is life and O'Neill is death. Both men were myth-makers and both sought God. In the search, both men failed, for their most mythic plays, *Lazarus Laughed* and *Back to Methuselah,* failed to convince. What does convince is not the quest both playwrights made for a twentieth-century divinity, but the life-seeking energy both men heartily espoused. Although O'Neill saw men as pitiable and felt that only in dope-dreams, drunkenness and physical death could they find relief from the squalid present, and although he came to feel that the only good lay in the communion of life-lies or in the memory of beatitude, he did not finally deny that life has value. In *The Iceman Cometh*, Hickey the salesman tries and fails to persuade the derelicts to give over the lie to rid themselves of illusion, to face the world and move up the evolutionary ladder from the bottom-of-the-sea Rathskeller in which they drift endlessly. Hickey's failure, the view that Hickey has brought death not life, is, indirectly, O'Neill's comment on Shaw's evolutionary beliefs. Men, the American held, will not change, and only in human sympathy can there be generated warmth and a sense of life. The Calibans who cry to dream again have little love for the Prosperos whose magic urges them out of the mud.

So brief a juxtaposition of the work of the leading playwrights is not sufficient even by implication to bring into comparison the drama of England and America in the twentieth century. Yet it is true that, despite the admiration extended them by theatre-arts advocates, John Galsworthy and Harley Granville-Barker were not imitated by the Americans. In later years there have been no playwrights in this country displaying such anger as John Osborne has in his protests at the way the Shavian life-force expends itself in nothing very much, like a lightning bolt striking the earth. Nor has Pinter's style found American imitators.

Rather what the American dramatists have revealed about the psychological and social context of their country has pointed to an inner darkness. Certainly other forces in the country have called with certitude for fully committed action in the strong light of virtuous purpose. But in the drama there has been a pervading bewilderment at a life that is too large, at matters that are too vast to attempt to control, and the regret for a lost life of value that yet hangs on the edges of memory.

O'Neill, the Boyg

My luncheon companion leaned across the table, peered at me through barely translucent glasses, and attacked: "I can't stand O'Neill!"

In the face of such a storm signal, I found it better to play the reed than the oak.

"Why?" I blandly asked.

"He's so long," she announced, "and so gloomy."

Such a neat summary of the case against Eugene O'Neill requires a lecture to refute. I tried a diversion instead.

"So is Wagner."

"I hate him too. They're both Boygs,* like in that awful Ibsen play. Long, gloomy, dark, and no fun whatever."

She may have had a point O'Neill's uncompromising determination to be (in the phrase he used when he applied for playwriting classes at Harvard) "an artist or nothing" is daunting to many who prefer to "go around," as the dark, mysterious Boyg commanded Peer Gynt to do in search of livelier company. Genius is never easy.

O'Neill's genius mystifies and sometimes causes resentment. It makes demands that audiences are understandably not always willing to pay. Yet even those who do not wish the association cannot entirely

---

*The "Boyg" is a symbol in Henrik Ibsen's Peer Gynt—a dark, formless, impalpable mass, which blocks Peer's flight and orders him to "go around" by a circuitous path on a voyage of self-discovery.

An introduction for a book publishing the papers presented by various scholars to a Eugene O'Neill conference at the University of Washington, Saint Louis, Missouri, 1988.

deny that genius is unmovably there, waiting, forcing those who cannot accept its unyielding presence to "go around."

Through most of the twentieth century in this country, O'Neill has overshadowed the path of theatrical development. Every American playwright has had to come to terms with his accomplishment, directly or indirectly. His theatrical certainties have forced themselves upon their work. His concerns have become with many variations theirs. His seriousness of purpose has been reflected in theirs. But pieties such as these can do little to still the opposition of persons like my luncheon companion. The antagonism toward O'Neill seems sometimes almost genetic in origin, impossibly difficult to extirpate.

It was not always so. Through the 1920's, an O'Neill opening was an Event, an occasion of national interest subjected to close scrutiny. His plays were received with impassioned praise by the faithful and were fiercely damned by the apostates. Knowledge of their content and style was sufficiently widespread so that they frequently received the accolade of parody by such masters as Ring Lardner, George S. Kaufman and Groucho Marx. Successful or not, there was no doubt that his plays were important and to be coped with. When for a time, after the failure of *Days Without End* in 1933, O'Neill disappeared from sight, the theatre, thinking he was played out, perhaps breathed more easily. Yet as Miller, Williams and Inge moved to their ascendency, his work remained a felt presence. The critic, George Jean Nathan, frequently growled that what the Broadway season needed was a new O'Neill play and spoke particularly of *The Iceman* Cometh, which he had read in manuscript. When that play was produced in 1946 and O'Neill "returned" to the theatre, the same sense of a special Event was present, but the Theatre Guild production was solemnly prestigious, and many in the post-war society found it tiresome. O'Neill himself had held it back from production during the war because he felt that at such a time a New York audience "could neither see nor hear its meaning."

It was at this point, as O'Neill's later plays were introduced, that O'Neill emerged as a Boyg. Ignoring the fact that actors eagerly seek to play the roles he created, ignoring the layer of rich comedy that illuminates the action of many of his plays, ignoring the skilled dialogue that falls so convincingly on the ear if not the eye, ignoring the freshness and seeming modernity of his stage techniques, some even yet resent having to enter the dark, deep waters of *The Iceman Cometh* or the fog-engulfed landscape of *Long Day's Journey into Night*. In his autobiography, Arthur Miller speaks perceptively of the "political consequences" of O'Neill's plays and of his "radical hostility to bourgeois civilization." Yet audiences do not regularly think of him as a political writer. He brought existential philosophy into the American theatre, but the first audiences for the Tao House plays, as he had prophesied, failed to understand their philosophical matrix.

Nevertheless, O'Neill, like all great playwrights, never failed to take his audiences seriously. He placed them where no escape was possible except by shameful flight through the lobby, forced them to become in a measure hypnotized, to enter deeply into his world, sometimes to drift as if they were drowning, and above all—no doubt to their surprise—to feel. The humanity of mankind is always at issue on his stage.

The noisy, the shallow, and the lost who do not want to be taken seriously are disturbed by power in the theatre. Richard Nixon's comment to Ruby Keeler after seeing her revival of *No, No, Nanette* sums the attitude exactly:

My wife and I of course like musical comedies. We like the theatre also. I don't mean by that they should always be old musicals, but I think this musical that they call escapist, I don't look at it that way. I think that after a long day most of us need a lift in the evening. I don't mean by that that sometimes I don't want to see a serious play or something of that sort.

A long day, indeed.

In 1988, people around the world paused to honor the centenary of O'Neill's birth. In his own country he has been celebrated with a variety of occasions of theatrical and critical importance. New London, Connecticut, commemorated him with a statue recalling his boyhood years along the banks of the Thames River where he lived as a child and young man. At various universities in New England, conferences, lectures and performances of his plays were offered. In New York City, a special "Theatre Committee for Eugene O'Neill" staged a birthday songfest of music from his plays and a retrospective of scenes played by many actors who had starred in his plays. On the west coast, near his California home, a range of revivals formed a theatrical concentrate of his work. Significant new productions were staged in San Francisco, Berkeley, Ashland and Seattle. An odds-on favorite on both coasts was a double bill of *Ah, Wilderness!* and *Long Day's Journey into Night* but other venturesome producers presented some of his earlier writings, among them *Marco Millions* by the American Conservatory Theatre of San Francisco and the four one-act plays of the S.S. *Glencairn,* staged on a ship in San Francisco Bay.

Abroad, scholarly and theatrical admirers joined forces in demonstrations that testified to the firmness of his reputation in foreign countries. Conferences in Stockholm, Brussels, Madrid, Nanjing and India were well attended by international audiences. Ingmar Bergman staged his first O'Neill play, *Long Day's Journey into Night,* for Dramaten, the Royal Swedish Theatre. In London a recent actor of "007" appeared as Con Melody in *Touch of the Poet.* In Shanghai *Mourning Becomes Electra* was offered, while in Nanjing, Chinese actors acquitted themselves in *Hughie.*

Publications in the centennial year were many, covering a variety of approaches: theatrical, historical, critical, the dramatist's letters, his unpublished or incomplete works and, at long last, through the agency of the Library of America, a definitive edition of all the finished dramas.

In sum, the world-wide celebrations formed a satisfactory tribute to the dramatist. Yet listening carefully, one could still hear the recalcitrant grumbling of those who remain unconvinced of O'Neill's power. Unanimity of appreciation is, of course, impossible to achieve, yet as O'Neill enters his second century, a different emphasis may lead to a difference in the appreciation he has so far gathered. To this point, O'Neill's life, the personal story to which *Long Day's Journey into Night* served as a Rosetta Stone, has dominated the criticism and production of his work. To read his life in his plays has been an essential beginning. Now, however, the shock of revelation has abated, and the game of tracing O'Neill's life in his art has become increasingly a trivial pursuit. Of coming importance is the study of O'Neill's art in itself. It is, after all, the art, more than the man with whom grumblers find fault. Until now, the art has been viewed largely in terms of its autobiographical revelations. Yet one of the few things that makes experiencing *Long Day's Journey into Night* bearable is the subliminal perception that one of the Tyrones survived, to become an "artist or nothing." In the next century perhaps scholars and critics will come increasingly to terms with the artistry of the plays themselves. To date there have been many excellent beginnings, but there is a far way yet to go to reveal the variety, the complexity, skill and multiple meanings of O'Neill's dramas. Similarly in the theatre there may evolve thoughtful restaging of the established masterpieces and further explorations into the possibilities of the plays that are less specifically autobiographical. Remembering that O'Neill always plays better than he reads, there may be some who trustingly will attempt works such as *Lazarus Laughed, Welded, Days Without End*, or *Dynamo*, which in its published form has never had a professional production.

There are many paths around the Boyg-like genius of O'Neill. So far only one path, the autobiographical, has led directly into that genius. In his second century, finding and following alternative routes to the center should be the direction and illumination the result.

Notes

Footnotes are keyed to the bibliography by a brief citation in capital letters and page number. Thus PLAYS I, 33 refers to Eugene O'Neill, *Complete Plays,* volume I, page 33.

The Seeking Flight

3   "She's starting to roll…" LETTERS 220

8   "I want to be…" LETTERS 26

9   "Then we knew…" Glaspell, Susan, *The Road to the Temple* (New York, Frederick A. Stokes, 1927) 254.

10 "…hold the family Kodak" Quoted in Deutsch, Helen and Stella Hanau, *The Provincetown* (New York, Farrar and Rinehart, Inc., 1931) 192.

11 "The sun, the hot sand…" PLAYS III, 812

14 "dig at the roots": "As Ever Gene," the Letters of Eugene O'Neill to George Jean Nathan, ed. Nancy L. Roberts and Arthur W. Roberts (Rutherford, NJ: Farleigh Dickinson University Press, 1987) 84. Hereafter NATHAN

From the Silence of Tao House

22 "Oh, I'm sure… " PLAYS III, 737

23 "All this talk…" PLAYS III, 788

24 "Pan in Logos!" PLAYS I, 285

25 "life is a solitary cell…" PLAYS II, 572

26 The medical records are in the library of the Eugene O'Neill Foundation, Tao House.

Birthday Greetings to Eugene O'Neill

O'Neill in Love

56 "It seems at times..." LETTERS 227

56 "you speak about fighting..." LETTERS 228

56 "Why are you taking..." EGO to Carlotta Monterey, January 12, 1927. BEINECKE

56 "I want so much..." LETTERS 234

57 "Dear there is nothing..." LETTERS 263

57 "I will be alone..." EGO to Carlotta Monterey, Nov. 7, 1927. BEINECKE

59 "STILL DRINKING" Wireless messages Jan. 3-13, 1929. BEINECKE

60 "Darling Fatbum..." LETTERS 356

60 "Your letters make…" LETTERS 36

61 "Darling One..." EGO to Carlotta Monterey O'Neill, Christmas, 1943, BEINECKE

62 "For the love of God..." LETTERS 579

Love's Labors Dispossessed

65 "fine, lovable people" The letters from O'Neill to Agnes Boulton O'Neill include those written between April 21 and May 2, 1921. Many of the letters are undated. HARVARD.

68 "An astonishing confession." Cf. COMMINS, pp. 22-26

72 "Excuse me for speaking..." LETTERS 269

73 "one of the great men," Cerf, Bennett, *At Random* (New York, Random House, 1977) 27

75 "She's sick..." COMMINS, p. 226

The Empowering Sea

81 "They cannot look..." Robert Frost, "Neither Out Far Nor In Deep."

81 "I never saw..." Emily Dickinson, "I never saw the sea."

83 "Heaved and heaved..." Herman Melville, *Moby Dick*, Chapter 51.

120 "gives life to..." PLAYS III, 570

122 "The whole business..." EGO to Lawrence Langner, Sept. 11, 1939. BEINECKE

122 "The World-Dictator fantasy..." EGO to Dudley Nichols, December 16, 1942. BEINECKE

Hughie

124 "presses suffocatingly upon..." PLAYS III, 847

124 "Only so many El trains..." PLAYS III, 838

124 "the whole damned city" PLAYS III, 837

124 "His mind has been..." PLAYS III, 846

124 "I wouldn't never worry..." PLAYS III, 849

125 "frantically as if..." PLAYS III, 844

125 "a saving revelation" PLAYS III, 850

125 "Beatific vision swoons..." PLAYS III, 848

Dreams of Joy, Dreams of Pain

129 "a paltry thing..." W. B. Yeats, "Sailing to Byzantium"

129 "I would have been..." PLAYS, III, 812

130 "a saint's vision..." PLAYS, III, 812

About a Touch of the Poet

136 "think may rewrite..." WORK DIARY, Feb. 16, 1942.

The Monastery and the Prison

138 "When he started..." Peck, Seymour, "A Talk with Mrs. O'Neill" *The New York Times*, Nov. 4, 1956

146 "his story-telling..." Miller, Arthur, *Timebends* (New York, The Grove Press, 1987), p. 244

146 [Sara] is too preoccupied..." PLAYS III, 393

147 "No you must allow..." PLAYS III, 392

147 "When you live through..." LETTERS 518

Bibliography

O'Neill, Eugene, *Complete Plays*, 3 vols, ed. Travis Bogard (New York: The Library of America, 1988) PLAYS

O'Neill, Eugene, *The Unknown O'Neill*, ed. Travis Bogard (New Haven, CT: Yale University Press, 1988)

O'Neill, Eugene, *The Calms of Capricorn*, 2 vols. ed. Donald Gallup (New Haven, CT: Yale University Library, 1981) CAPRICORN

O'Neill, Eugene, *Poems, 1912-1942*, ed. Donald Gallup (New Haven, CT: Yale University Library, 1979) POEMS

O'Neill, Eugene, *Inscriptions: Eugene O'Neill to Carlotta Monterey O'Neill*, (New Haven CT: Privately printed, 1960)

O'Neill, Eugene, Work Diary, 1924-1941. 2 vols. Transcribed by Donald Gallup (New Haven CT: Yale University Library, 1981) WORK DIARY

"The Theatre We Worked For..." The Letters of Eugene O'Neill to Kenneth Macgowan, ed. Jackson R. Bryer and Travis Bogard (New Haven, CT: Yale University Press, 1982) MACGOWAN

"Love, and Admiration and Respect," the O'Neill Commins Correspondence, ed. Dorothy Commins (Durham, NC: Duke University Press, 1986) COMMINS

"As Ever, Gene," the Letters of Eugene O'Neill to George Jean Nathan, ed. Nancy L. Roberts and Arthur W. Roberts (Rutherford, NJ: Farleigh Dickinson University Press, 1987) NATHAN

Selected Letters of Eugene O'Neill, ed. Travis Bogard and Jackson R. Bryer (New Haven, CT: Yale University Press, 1988) LETTERS

Bogard, Travis, Richard Moody, Walter J. Meserve, *The Revels History of Drama in English, vol. viii, American Drama.* (London: Methuen & Co., Ltd., 1977)

Gelb, Arthur and Barbara Gelb, *O'Neill.* (New York, NY: Harper and Bros., 1962, rev. 1974)

Sheaffer, Louis, *O'Neill, Son and Playwright.* (Boston, MA: Little Brown, 1968)

Sheaffer, Louis, *O'Neill, Son and Artist.* (Boston, MA: Little Brown, 1973) SHEAFFER

Special Collections

The Berg Collection, New York Public Library. BERG

The Beinecke Rare Book and Manuscript Library, Yale University, New Haven CT. BEINECKE

The Harvard Theatre Collection, The Houghton Library, Harvard University, Cambridge, MA. HARVARD